Saddles East

*Horseback over the old Oregon
Trail*

by

John W. Beard

The Long Riders' Guild Press

www.thelongridersguild.com

ISBN: 1-59048-042-2

To my wife,

THE FINEST COMPANION THAT EVER RODE

THE TRAILS OF LIFE WITH HER MAN

CONTENTS

I

PREPARING FOR THE LONG RIDE

ONE OF THE MOST STIMULAT-
ing things about any journey is the preparation for it before-
hand. Anticipation may even out-joy realization, and we had
almost two years of busy preparation crammed with consuming
interest and with enjoyment.

Into my study came two gorgeous saddles, made to order and
hand stamped, planned and prepared for the coming ride.
They were made by the George Lawrence Company of Portland, Oregon, skilled saddle makers. They were almost a year
in the making. They were Western, Do Di Ho, fourteen
inches wide, undercut for leg room, cantle three and one-half
inches high with Cheyenne Roll, three-quarter rigged, with
dees laced in. In short, they were and are the very perfection
of the saddle makers's art.

Anticipation was thrilling while these saddles were in the
making, and possession has but added to our joy. There is ever
a thrill in possessing a perfect thing. Haunting the factory and
eagerly watching as flower after flower blossomed into full
glory under the skilled hands of the master artists, we came
to love the very pungent odor and tang of the leather and to
admire the men who made these saddles possible for us.

We spent many happy hours together as we shopped for ac-
cessories such as bridles, martingales, spurs, lariats, saddle
blankets. We were especially anxious to secure martingales
that were not only classy but that were really strong, for many
horses have a nasty habit of rearing up and falling over back-
ward and a good, strong martingale would help to keep the
animal's head where it belonged.

Our next care was the selection of spurs. A rider on the
long way we were to take must be the master of his horse on
every step of the journey. Spurs, when rightly used, always
help the rider to gain and keep that mastery. A horse seems to
be able to think of only one thing at a time and when he is
thinking of devilment it is wise to try the expulsive power of
a new thought. A touch of the spurs will help him to change

1

his mind. Spurs are not cruel unless the man who uses them is brutal. It is only the brutal man who rides with "rowels dyed in blood." Such a man should never ride.

Well, we examined every make and style of spur that we could find, from the little, stubby, military plaything made to grace the dapper boot of the army officer when in full dress uniform to the dainty wheel with vicious, needle-sharp points. We finally decided on the old-fashioned cowboy's kind, made of heavy stainless steel, inlaid with silver ornaments and with long, pointed spikes radiating from a circular disk.

The decision in favor of this type was made when we remembered how on the ranch as a boy, if the riding got too tough, we would dig the long spikes into the corded cinch and practically tie ourself in the saddle long enough to ride out the storm. Now, we will have to admit that when we felt them buckled on our high-heeled boots, sent up as a present by our son from a California ranch, we felt equal to taking a chance on "Ten Minutes to Midnight," or even old "Midnight" himself.

We were also greatly concerned about our saddle blankets. We wanted them thick enough and soft and pliant enough effectively to cushion the heavy stock saddles. Saddle sores are cruel and crippling things, and should be avoided at any cost. We wanted to take the same horses clear through. Then, we wanted color, real color, so we secured three of bright red wool, striped and checked in white. They were so clamant that we often remarked that they would make beautiful kilties. Their brilliant colors looked surprisingly fitting on the coal-black horses.

The army saddle would probably have been easier on the horses as it is much lighter, but the Western Stock Saddle is always easier on the rider, and with good saddle blankets both horse and rider were thus well prepared.

If selecting and securing of the saddles was an interesting experience, the buying of the horses was much more so. In fact, it was a short course not only in horse anatomy but also in human nature. I answered almost every advertisement that appeared in the two daily papers of horses for sale. I found some of the horses too young, some of them too old, some of them too slender and delicate for such a task as carrying the heavy load of saddle and rider over two thousand five hundred miles. Some of them were well adapted to pull the plough or drag the harrow across the fields but hardly light enough to walk, trot, run up and down a mountain trail.

One was advertised as a "gentle riding horse for a woman or child," but when she was ridden, it was by a trained rider brought over from a riding academy, and it required all her strength and skill to keep from exchanging her seat in the saddle for one on the wet Oregon turf. Another, a large, fine-looking buckskin was recommended as being "without flaw and blemish," but I found that it was almost impossible for him to go straight down hill; he would only descend on the oblique; something was radically wrong with one of his shoulders.

One had four highly polished hoofs, but upon close inspection one hoof was found to be split clear to the hair line; the split had been filled with some kind of plaster and all highly polished. Another had beautiful lines, was young and full of life. The lady who was selling her assured me she was as "gentle as a kitten." I stooped down to pick up her left front foot when she lashed out with her left hind foot, landing it on my hip, where I maintained no gentle horse should ever kick a gentleman. So I passed her by.

Still another, a splendid little gray, seemed almost ideal as a mount for Mrs. Beard. She was perfect in form and action and with bright, sparkling eyes, but with an abominable spirit. An old negro had the horse under his care. She was saddled up and a stable boy mounted her to put her through her paces around a small pasture. I noted that the boy gingerly mounted her and I could detect a slight humping of her back and always he held the reins in one hand and the saddle horn gripped tightly in the other. As he was bringing her back I said to the old darky, "Now, Dad, give me the low-down on that horse. Is she suitable for my wife to ride?"

He looked at me with great, solemn eyes and said, "Does you love that wife, Boss?"

"More than I do my life."

"Well, Boss, you better buy another horse."

Nevertheless I was so charmed with the little ball of gray

fire that I asked to try her out. Mounting her, I rode her through the pasture and down the road a short distance, then turned her around and rode her back. As we came to the gate I urged her to go on by, but she was of another turn of mind, and rearing high into the air swung around. Again I urged her forward and, thinking that I had reined her a little too firmly, I let the reins loosen just a trifle and down went her head. As her head went down she went up on all fours and simply exploded. I managed by some hook or crook to stay on her, but when it was finally over I found that the saddle horn had given me such a blow in the groin that I would feel the hurt for some time to come.

As I turned the reins of the little witch back to the old negro, I said, "You were right, Dad, a man who loves his wife would hardly buy this horse."

"Yas sir, Boss, yas sir," said he, "she can surely work up action quick."

"At least," I said to myself, "here is one honest man."

Well, as I remarked before, he who buys a horse will learn a lot of horse anatomy and a lot about human nature.

After a long search I found the two I wanted.

A fine black filly, with a blazed face and with white bobby socks on the two hind legs, was advertised for sale. The moment I saw her I knew she was the horse I wanted for Mrs. Beard to ride. I liked the looks of the woman who was selling her. The price seemed right and the bargain was soon made. The purchase was made in January and I was to take possession on July 28, 1947.

When she was brought in for inspection there came along with her another horse — a big black gelding, with a white spot in his forehead. He also took my fancy but the good owner seemed somewhat reluctant to sell him or even talk about selling him. It came out, however, that some one of her relatives was a preacher and her observations had been that a good preacher was not necessarily a good horseman. And it soon appeared that she had a real feeling of kindness for a minister and had no intention of selling him a bunch of living dynamite. She wanted no preacher's blood upon her hands. So at first she refused to sell this big black horse with the white star in his forehead.

When I finally assured her I was willing to take the risk and my blood would not be upon her hands, we struck the bargain, the same price as for the filly.

And was I proud and did I have a job on my hands? He was a living, throbbing ball of dynamite and he was so renamed. At the barn of the Western Riders Association, where I kept him for seven months after our first summer's ride, they called him the "Widow Maker."

My son wanted me to shoot him, and a son on a cattle ranch in California offered to send me the finest saddle horse on the place, a magnificent buckskin. But I loved the very devilshness of the black and he carried me as few horses could, and without a limp, over the two thousand five hundred miles of the Old Oregon Trail.

Every morning when we saddled up we had an argument whether I was going to ride him or whether he was going to ride me, but always there was a link of friendship between us, and when I would put my head out of the tent door in the morning, he would always greet me with a friendly neigh and I always gave him the first helping of the precious oats.

Now, it had been a real task, and at times what seemed to be a hopeless task, to secure the right kind of horses for the journey. But the rest of the preparation was just sheer happiness.

Every summer for forty years of our work in the ministry and of our married life, we had spent a month camping, living out under the skies like Indians. We knew camp life and we knew how to be comfortable in rain, hail, snow or ice.

We knew now the things we needed. So we soon had our miner's tent, seven feet square at the base and some seven feet to the top of the jointed center pole, with a good thick floor-cloth sewed in and with bobbinet front for the door. The air mattresses and the down sleeping bags assured us comfort in any kind of weather.

For cooking utensiles we decided to take our old well-tried camping outfit — a nested set of dishes, cups and plates of tin, two small pails, a coffee pot, knives and forks of the lightest weight, a small frying pan with its long, rigid handle, a small wire grill with four folding legs to be pushed into the

ground over the fire pit. With these we were all finally set for
the great trek.

When the two panniers, which had been made to our own
order, were packed ready for the journey, they weighed about
one hundred pounds each. The load considered as average for a
pack horse is two hundred pounds. So our conscience was easy.
With a 32 Special Winchester Carbine for the saddle of Old
Dynamite, to be taken along for use just in case we might get
lost in a mountain pass or out on the desert and need to sup-
plement our food with a jack rabbit or even an antelope, we
were ready for the start.

That is, we were ready as far as the material preparation
was concerned. And we were somewhat ready in the more
serious preparation of mind and heart. We had been making
such preparation for years.

The Old Oregon Trail through the valleys of the Platte
and the Snake from Independence, Missouri, to Seaside, Oregon, had become my own. We really own only that which we
love and I had learned to love that trail. I had ridden it time
and time again and that without going out of my study.

In the study a great map hangs whereon are ranges of lofty
mountains in black extending from north to south, with an oc-
casional gap between the heights inviting one to come and go
through. Here and there are patches of blue, the lakes, that
say, "Look, the places to camp and rest when the saddle is
hard and the horses are tired and the rider is weary." And
here are bright, red lines where the trails have gone. There
is one, broad and red and solid and zigzag which takes its
way straight from southeast to northwest, and crosses many
blue lines that wander in mazy motion, little blue lines of
rivers, just the place to pause and water the stock.

Up in one corner, under a big ox yoke, is the legend telling
that the broad, solid, red line is that of the Old Oregon
Trail. In the middle of the map goes a covered wagon with
four oxen pulling it; on the sides are many of the real makers
of the trail, buffalo and antelope and gray wolves and grizzly
bears and Indians mounted on splendid horses — all looking
curiously on.

Yes, many, many times here in the study, the swivel chair
has become a saddle, and the drawn-out leaves of the desk be-

come stirrups, and thus mounted, I have ridden back and forth and up and down the old loved trail as pictured on the map. It is mine. It belongs to me. And I often prepared, in imagination, to ride it in fact.

When all the plans were finally perfected, and we knew that we would soon be on the move, we began intensively to inform our minds and indurate our hearts and harden our bodies at the expense of study in theology perhaps. We got out the *Journals of Lewis and Clark* and read them from beginning to end, and it was just like visiting the old familiar places. Francis Parkman's *Oregon Trail* was once more devoured with greedy avidity. Irving's *Astoria* kept us pursuing the thrilling tale into the wee hours of many a night. *The Adventures of Captain Bonneville* by the same author came next. *The Great Salt Trail* by Inman and Cody was followed through word by word. Every draught of these volumes made us thirsty for more and more. What magic hours and nights Mrs. Beard and I spent together reading, preparing our minds to find, to pass over, and to enjoy that which had become for us the enchanted way.

We did not stop our quest for information by our reading but we visited every historic spot which time let us visit. We went down and stood by the rock cairn where Lewis and Clark and Sacajawea made their salt that winter of 1805-06 near Seaside, Oregon. Yes, the old rocks are still there, and the same pounding waves, and the moaning of the winds over the waters, which perhaps made them sick for home as they gathered around the fires glowing beneath the steaming kettles. A strange nostalgia came into our hearts as we stood there, and in imagination rekindled their fires that have long since gone out.

We visited the grassy acres by the river where Fort Clatsop was built for their winter quarters. Archeologists have found few remains, the eyes see none. Time eats with greedy fangs into every fabric man can make; it has fastened it's relentless teeth upon the Old Trail itself and has shaken it around it's grizzled head, leaving mere traces here and there. In another hundred years perhaps every vestige will have disappeared.

From Seaside to Fort Vancouver is something like a hundred miles but we passed that way again and, looking eagerly over the scar where an excavacation had been made to recover the outline of the foundations of the old fort, we picked up some bits of blue plate which once may have been the pride of Margaret McLoughlin, the wife of the White Headed Eagle. This blue plate sent us to Oregon City, that historic place by the falls of the Willamette, and to the church of St. Johns where John McLoughlin and Margaret were sleeping. They have since been removed to a final resting place high on the hill.

Then up Willamette Valley, past the falls, and near Woodburn turned west to Gervais to the church of St. Louis. There says a small, bronze tablet inserted in the floor, "Wih-munke Waken (Holy Rainbow) sleeps in peace beneath."

Wih-munke Waken was the wife of Dorion, the interpreter, who came with the Wilson Price Hunt expedition to Astoria in 1811-12.

With that expedition we know were sixty men, two children, and this devoted Indian woman. There is a stone marker along the trail, near Powder River, and it bears her name and the words, "Just east of here, Mrs. Dorion gave birth to a child, December 30, 1811." We know that after the time of travail on this desperate winter's day, Madame Dorion resumed the terrible journey into the west.

At the church where Madame Dorion lies sleeping, an old priest is still ministering. His parish, once the largest in all of Oregon, is now one of the smallest. The old priest is very feeble but he carries on his service of God at the altars.

Pleasant was our visit and, when he knew that we were to undertake the long, hard ride across half the continent on horseback, he wished the blessing of God upon us.

From Madame Dorion's resting place beneath the floor of that little Catholic Church, it is but a short way, as cars go today, to the place of Jason Lee's early Methodist Mission.

From these shrines we turned our feet and minds toward the little white, slender-steepled Presbyterian Church out on Tualatin Plains. We sought there the last resting place of an old Mountain Man, an old beaver trapper, an old guide, one whose name, like that of Kit Carson and Jim Bridger, is known over every stretch of desert or mountain pass of the west; and yet one whom we have come to regard as one of the first citizens of the early days, Joseph L. Meek. We found his grave and its marker.

It was an atmosphere of peace and rest that we found there in that little churchyard. The good pastor had mowed the grass and tenderly pruned the shrubs and nursed the flowers. One felt it a blessing just to be there and walk it's sacred paths in the quiet of the evening hour. And we took off our hats and said a prayer for the Old Mountain Man who got religion and found a resting place for his tired feet, and peace at last.

Going out of that cemetery, leaving behind that handful of dust sleeping beneath the grass and flowers, we were glad that we were soon to pass over the plains where he had adventured, and over the long trail that he helped to make.

Back again on the highway, we found the almost deserted village of Barlow, and near Barlow the somewhat neglected cemetery and the place of the grave of Samuel Barlow, the man who hewed through the mighty forest south of Mt. Hood, the Barlow Road, which bears his name.

The last and one of the most difficult sections of the Old Oregon Trail passed over this land. Barlow was a man of dauntless courage. One of his sayings is a western classic: "God never made a mountain that He did not make a place for a man to go over it or around it, if he could find the place. I am going to hunt for that place."

Joel Palmer in his diary tells us when his wagon train arrived at The Dalles that some sixty families were waiting for a passage down the river, that there were but two small boats running down to Cascade Falls, and that chances to get down were very limited.

These conditions confronted the intrepid Barlow. His part of a wagon train had halted out of The Dalles at the Five Mile Creek. Here the party made the start for the low pass south of Mt. Hood. In that party were nineteen men and women, besides children. They had seven horses, thirteen wagons, sixteen yoke of oxen, and a single dog. On the first day of October, with his watchword, "On, on," Barlow started. The bullwhack cracked and the creaking, groaning wagons began to roll along the last, hard march. It seems that at the end of the first day they were at the Tygh Valley. If so, it was surely a good day's march. When Fremont with his pack train of some hundred horses, twenty-five men and with Indians guides, made this march on November 25 and 26, 1843, he made it in about the same length of time.

The way around and over the mountains and through the mighty forests that cover all the valleys and slopes was a hard and cruel way. It was especially difficult and trying across the White River and down the mountain side at Klip Creek and dread Laurel Hill. They did not get the wagons through that winter. But all the party did get through except Rector, who, on account of the delicate health of his wife, turned back and took the river route. They rested and refreshed themselves with food, secured at the Philip Foster place, arriving in Oregon City for their Christmas dinner.

The next year, 1846, Barlow and his men with saw and axe cleared a road through these same mountains for all who came after him to follow. Today, all around his last resting place are the broad and fertile fields since brought into cultivation and high production. When we visited his grave the sun was setting and had turned the fields of wheat into a shimmering carpet of gold, a picture of what the labors of such men as Joel Palmer, William Rector, and Samuel Barlow have given to our day and generation.

II

THE BARLOW ROAD

The Barlow Road was the last and hardest stretch along the Old Trail. On this road many marks of the Trail can still be found. Since one riding into the sunrise must needs go this way, we decided to cover this hundred miles first, as a conditioning trip for our full journey the following spring. Whoever rides this part of the trail should cover it in the months of July and August, because of the snows and storms of any other season. We started on the twenty-eighth day of July, 1947.

On the morning of the twenty-eighth, we brought the two saddle horses in from their pasture near the Oregon Ship Yards, some eleven miles, at the northwestern corner of the city. It was a task. The horses were unaccustomed to the dense traffic and frantically afraid of trucks, so we had a real job of riding whenever a truck went by. However, we arrived safely at the manse in time to eat lunch, get into our riding togs and be off at one o'clock.

At Eighty-Second Avenue we picked up our pack horse, Black Dust, a round roly-poly animal of about eleven hundred pounds weight, but so short and so round that it was with great difficulty we could keep the pack on his back. He had an inferiority complex so pronounced that he would try to kick the saddle horses every time the opportunity offered. Many an opportunity offered over the mountain riding of a month.

With Black Dust we had many an interesting time. The first incident, and it threatened to end the trip somewhat early, came when, on the highway halfway between Portland and Oregon City, a carload of hilarious youths came speeding up with a "Hi-ho Silver," brushed by, scraping the pannier. The packhorse, frightened, began to pitch. A fishing rod and a few other utensile that had not been too securely tied on went flying in several directions. The packhorse slipped and fell on the wet road and was almost run over by a fast speeding car that followed the first. Before I could dismount and sit on his head till the load could be released, he had pounded his head into bloody bumps, but soon with the help of a lad who knew horses and loved them well, the panniers were removed, the animal was on his feet, the load was replaced, and we were again on the way. The damage was not great, but it did make us more watchful about cars for the rest of the ride that day .

Our first night's camp was in the rodeo grounds at Oregon

City, near the old emigrant crossing of Abernathy Creek, near where lie buried the Indians who had killed the Whitmans and who had been hanged by Joe Meek. Here was history close at hand. Long we lay awake, looking up at the pale moon and pondering the fact that much of the so called progress we call civilization has come through blood and tears and over the broken bodies of men.

The next morning we followed the example of the early emigrant by getting rid of all surplus baggage. A tent, two army cots, two pairs of heavy hiking boots, two divided skirts, and two shirts were rolled into a single package and stored away in Oregon City's Municipal Garage. After breakfast of bacon, eggs and black coffee, we were actually on our way back over the historic Barlow Road, the Oregon Trail's western end.

Out past the rambling, old colonial building on the Holcomb Place where early freighters were accustomed to get their meals, we went and arrived at the end of the day at the Philip Foster ranch, a donation land claim, highly cultivated in the early days. The first travelers over the Barlow Road were always happy to reach this hospitable farmstead, for here they were assured of a hearty welcome and supplies that all would surely need. Here we received such a welcome as only the pioneers or sons and daughters of pioneers know how to give.

We helped with the evening chores and were especially happy that we still knew, without the aid of our compass, which side of the cow to approach for the highly technical exercise of milking.

We drank out of the well dug a hundred years ago by Philip Foster. How cool and refreshing the clear, cold water and how lovingly the lilac bushes, that had been brought around the Horn, hung over the wall. We sat up most of the night, the hours spent with the granddaughter, Mrs. Meyers, and her husband, Ray, being too precious to waste in sleep.

It was with the reverence one would feel in handling some rare jewel or ancient book, that we took in our hands the rolling pin made of rosewood, brought also around the Horn; a pair of gold scales, used in the excitement of '49; and the little old kettle which Philip Foster was accustomed to take on his hunting trips in which to cook the few potatoes he carried with him. And we handled the gun, his old reliable meat supplier. Mrs. Beard was fascinated with the old-fashioned dress which Mrs. Foster had worn in 1843, and did not hesitate to put it on at the first invitation. The dress was quaint and really beautiful and lost nothing of its dainty loveliness on the new model.

Perhaps the most interesting thing of all was to hold in our hands the very letters which John McLoughlin had written; business letters, but now romantic and priceless with the accumulated gold of the years.

Here we also began to know something of the pathos and the heartbreaks that came to the followers of the early trail; something of the hunger and the thirst and the hardships that left many little sacred mounds of earth on every mile of its way. Here we heard the story of little Nancy Black, a child who all along the endless trek had hungered for fresh vegetables and fruit. Arriving at the Foster ranch she had eaten too freely of the luscious fruits of the orchard, and after a brief illness had been laid to rest in the plot of ground under the solemn trees on the hill above.

On the long trail next year we were to find many a marked grave where young and old alike had grown tired and had laid them down to sleep long before they had come in to the land of their dreams.

Yes, the trail was marked by many a grave, some have said as many as seventeen on every mile across the plains.

Leaving the historic Philip Foster Ranch, we passed through the town of Sandy, and down into the Sandy River at the spot where young William Barlow in his effort to get through and secure food and help for the hungry company left behind in the mountains, had cut down a sapling and with this as his vaulting pole had leaped from rock to rock to cross the stream, then in spate. Then up the long, narrow ridge we went over the well-named Devil's Backbone, on through what was left of Marmot, once a post office established in 1886 on the old trail with F. S. Peake as the first postmaster, but now just a tumbledown log cabin with a few rotting specimens of animals and birds collected and mounted by Adolf Ashoff, an old guide, forester and lover of the creatures of the woods and all outdoor things.

If one would see the wreck which time makes of all the works and hopes of man, let him go up this long, narrow ridge called the Devil's Backbone, let him pause at this place called Marmot, let him pull aside the tangle of vines and briars, step carefully upon the rotten boards of the porch, look through the holes in the walls which had once been windows, gaze at the floor littered with the musty papers and bits of broken furniture and moth-eaten forms that had once been lithe, active graceful creatures of the forest and he will feel the chill, icy breath of time in his very soul. He will not want to stay long, but he will want to be up and away and doing and living to the full every minute which we call now.

We ourselves did not tarry long at Marmot. Even the horses seemed to want to be away and moved out with a speed hard to control. We soon reached the Odell Ranch and went into camp in a secluded, grassy spot on the bank of the river. This was one of the stopping places along the Barlow Road, where flocks and herds and horses could be corralled for the night. Here we heard the story of a great fir tree, which, when felled and split into boards, had yielded many arrow heads and bullets.

From the Odell Ranch the trail passed through Rhododendron, through Toll-gate and up over Laurel Hill, a place rightfully dreaded by the early traveler, and down which, as William Barlow said so expressively, "We went like shots off a shovel." Now the rider of the trail will pass over this section on a fine bridle path, constructed by the Government, pass by an abandoned mine shaft, over the slide rock above the steep-sided canyon, go on past Government Camp and down into Summit Meadows in perfect safety and through breathtaking scenery.

In the Summit Meadows we camped two days. The grass was so abundant, the water of the clear, singing creek was so pure and cold, the flowers were so bright and colorful, and old Mt. Hood was so majestic and so serene there above us, it seemed we could have camped for an eternity in perfect peace and contentment. At night, as we sat by our campfire, near to the parcel of ground fenced in with pickets where lie some of the early dead, and knew that they had died just short of their journey's end, we felt that they had not died, they had just been translated. They had come into their Promised Land a little sooner than they had expected.

Nowhere on earth would they have found a more fitting resting place. There was majestic, snow-mantled Hood above them. There were the meadows colored with the Indian paint brush around them. In the winter time the snows would cover them with a blanket all soft and white and warm. And in the spring the gentle, mellow music of the winds going through the trees would play for them. Who could look for couch more magnificent? We talked little that night but sat and thought of the time when, as boy and girl, we had started down the long trail together.

By the time we had arrived at Summit Meadows, old Tom, the airdale, had developed tender feet. Next morning, after washing them in soap and water and massaging them with cold cream, we were again on the trail, up past the grave of an unknown pioneer woman, pausing only long enough to look at the old ruts, still plainly visible, where the Barlows had first crossed the Salmon River some hundred yards to the north.

Past Buzzard's Point we went where an impressive view of Hood must have thrilled the weary emigrant, down through the Devil's Half-Acre (why it was so named is a mystery, for it looks more like an angel's paradise, with its abundant grass and clear mountain stream, garlanded with Indian paint brush and a myriad of other flowers) we traveled on to Grindstone, a triangular opening in the woods, just roomy enough for picketing the horses on their thirty-foot ropes, near a little spring. We prepared to remain here over the Sabbath Day. We soon made camp, cleaned out the spring, spread our sleeping bags beneath the thick, widely spreading branches of a giant fir and turned in for a long night's rest.

Scarcely had we pulled the flaps of the down bag over our shoulders when there came a tremendous crash of thunder, rolling its bellowing echoes through all the mountains. A flash of lightning illuminated the entire forest. The rain now began

to fall gently, but under the thick branches of the fir scarcely
a drop reached us, and those that did slid harmlessly off the
water-repellant envelope in which the sleeping bags were
encased.

Lying there under the giant tree, whose growth was of a
hundred years or more, and whose branches were spread out
over us like a mother's love, we could really appreciate the
power, the awe, the grandeur of the mountain storm. But even
thunder and lightning may become common, and we soon forgot both in dreamless sleep.

We spent the Sabbath Day washing the few necessary things,
mending some broken places on the pack saddle, and looking
for signs of the Old Trail. We found real blazes on two giant
firs. They were so deep that they might well have been made by
Barlow and Rector when they scouted out the trail over a hundred years ago.

Monday morning we were up and away, bright and early,
at five o'clock and off by eight, for by nightfall we wanted to
reach Gate, the place where the Old Trail entered the forest,
and where toll was collected on the east end of the road.

We pressed steadily on all day, pausing only to rest the
horses after some steep climb. Down Barlow Creek we went,
past the old Klinger Place, over White River, down into Klip
Creek, up the steep incline where the going had been exceeding-
ly laborious and dangerous for the pioneer wagons, past Faith
Springs, past Emigrant Springs. We would camp at Emigrant
Springs on our way back. Just as the sun was setting, we came to
the tumbledown ruins that had been called Gate.

The gulch was dark and lonesome, and, in trying to find
wider stretches of meadow where we could picket the horses,
we passed some rugged and dangerous going. However, being
assured by a rancher that this was the historic place we had been
seeking, we camped for the night.

Here we experienced some of the many things that can make
an · exploring trip really interesting. First, Old Dynamite
stepped on the airedale and the gathering shadows were filled
with the yelping and crying of a badly hurt dog. Then Dynamite and the packhorse got into an awful battle and it seemed
they might kill each other or, at least, break some legs before
they could be separated.

While going about the task of preparing the evening camp, a story of two men, who had been murdered there on an early day, kept coming to my mind. I had been told that their graves were a short way above us in the gulch. As the tale came to me it was of a father and son who came to the Gate in the evening and had camped at first with some Indians, but becoming fearful, had moved to a place where two white men were camped. Suspicious that these two men were desperate characters, they had moved a second time farther up the gulch, where in the morning they had been found murdered.

That was the story I had heard. It may have been only a myth but there in the gathering darkness of the gulch the tale took on a sinister meaning and the haunting question, "Who killed those men?" kept coming to my mind as the work of the camp was pursued. I would drive down a picket pin, pause and ask myself, "Who killed those men?" Then I would drive down the second and the third and, after each, would ask the question, "Who killed those men?" As I gathered wood for the fire, cooked the bacon and eggs and made the coffee, always the question came, "Who?" With work all done, dishes washed, the sleeping bags pulled around us, the question, "Who, who, who?" kept coming to my mind. Finally sleep came. But in the middle of the night, I awakened, my hands moist, great drops of sweat on my forehead, and up in a tree above us a big, bright-eyed hoot owl, and he too, was asking the question, "Who, who, who?" This had awakened me. I felt like using the carbine on him, but used only the flash light, and he was off and away. I have asked myself many a time since, "Who?" but have never had an answer. What a night!

When we broke camp next morning we found the airedale somewhat lame, and knowing the road to Tygh Valley would be too long for him to walk, he was placed on the back of Black Dust, the packhorse, who showed his displeasure in no mistakable way. But in due time we arrived in the Valley of the Tygh and camped on the very edge of the clear, crystal stream among the cottonwoods.

How women love to wash! Almost as soon as we said, "Whoa," to the horses, we were at home and the limbs of the cottonwoods were gorgeous as a carnival with blue Levis, red bandanna handkerchiefs, scarfs, dish cloths, towels and sundry, waving like pennants in the wind.

Old Tom, the airedale, being quite sore and stiff and the camp by the stream so inviting, we decided to stay over for a day. Again we washed and anointed his feet, spread out the rubber poncho for his couch and left him sleeping in the shade while we explored the Valley of the Tygh.

Here Barlow had come at the end of his first day's travel from Five Mile Creek near The Dalles. He had crossed the stream and rested here before he made the steep climb with his wagon to the plateau above.

Looking across the bronze hills to the north, one may still see the ruts of the old road where he came down to the valley. Looking up the canyon walls to the south and west, one can see where the steep climb out was made.

It is said that the valley at that time was a sea of waving grass reaching to the bellies of the oxen; that the stream, full and crystal clear, was teeming with trout, an ideal place for a home in the west. Barlow must have been tempted to call it a trek; unyoke his oxen; build his cabin; but a dream was in his heart and he followed it to the end. His heart had long since gone before to the Valley of the Willamette and he was dedicated to pay, if necessary, with his body for his soul's desire.

Had he stopped in the Valley of the Tygh, his name would perhaps be unknown, but today it is common throughout the coast country, and the old Barlow Road will be known to countless thousands yet unborn.

Leaving the Valley of the Tygh, we rode on toward The Dalles, taking part of two days for the journey that Barlow had made in one. We left old Tom behind, as it seemed needless to make him suffer the agonies of the long walk and his riding on the packhorse was not a great success. We camped at Eight Mile Creek and did our Boy Scout deed for the day by putting out a fire that threatened to destroy the home of an old couple on whose place we had planned to stay for the night.

The next day we passed the place at Five Mile Creek where Barlow had started his journey, and came on into The Dalles. Here we were royally entertained by Bill Dent, the blind mayor of the city. He is a remarkable man and, in spite of his handicap, has made a success of life such as few men ever attain.

At Pulpit Rock, where Jason Lee had preached to the Indians, the horses got into a brawl so vicious that the very fiends of darkness must have laughed. However, we were not greatly disturbed, for we had completed the first stage of the journey.

Now we turned our horses back over the trail. We picked up the airedale at the Tygh. He was in fine shape and boisterously glad to have us back. A few days later he was struck by a rattler and finally died from the effects of the bite, though we were able to bring him home.

We stopped at Emigrant Springs, a storied spot in an open place of about an acre, in the very heart of the forest, where only a few giant firs are growing. Here from the spring, some four or five feet in diameter and four or five feet deep, the emigrant found an abundance of clear, pure, cold water. Here he loved to rest.

On the last day of our journey we brought our horses in fifty miles, confident now that we could ride the Old Oregon Trail clear through from this end in the sunset to its other end in the sunrise on the banks of theMissouri.

Now we began to prepare in real earnest for that ride. We took special "Setting up" exercises every day. We practiced mounting and dismounting on the saddles, which were placed on dummy horses in the basement. We went twice a week to the Western Riders Association, where our horses were stabled, and rode for the entire morning. We set up our tent in the yard, equipped it with air mattresses and down sleeping bags, and through the month of March slept out through rain and storm.

We now felt duly prepared and well qualified in spirit, mind and body actually to make our life-long dream come true — to take saddles east and ride into the sunrise.

III

THE TRAIL TO WASCOPAM

At ten o'clock, a.m. April first, a bright spring morning, we were out at the Western Riders Association, mounted and eager to be away. Old Black Dyna-

mite was a prancing bunch of muscles, a throbbing bunch of
nerves, ready for a bucking spree, a roping contest, or a running race, or for the two thousand five hundred mile journey
that lay ahead. He was set for anything that had action in it,
pulling on the reins, champing on the bit, foaming at the
mouth, stamping impatiently. Black Fairy, the new saddle
horse, was just as anxious to be off, making it rather hard for
Mrs. Beard, her rider, to say good-by to the numerous friends
who had come out to see us off.

Black Diamond, the saddle horse of last year, now conscript-
ed as pack horse, was making it hard for all concerned. She was
mad all over. She showed her resentment by biting and kicking
everything that came near her.

Roan Eagle, a big, strong gelding of some twelve hundred
pounds, who had been bought and trained for the hard job of
carrying the duffel and who tried to tear down the barn when
brought in, had to be sent back to the ranch for more definite
training. We put Black Diamond in his place and secured Black
Fairy for the other saddle horse.

The new horse proved to be about as sweet a little mount as
one could find. She was just three years old, fast as the wind and
with action as quick and springy as a cat's. She was seemingly
tireless. She never strayed far from camp and when called in
the early morning would lift her head with an answering neigh
and trot up for feed. This, of course, always brought the other
two horses so we never had trouble catching them.

If the horses were anxious to be off so were their masters.
Through almost a life time we had looked forward to this hour.
Now we were ready to go, bedecked with spurs, chaps, blue
Levis, and red wool shirts, a gift from the Pendleton Woolen
Mills, through the kindness of C. C. Wintermute. We
said good-by to Walter Meacham, the members of the Oregon
Trail Association, and a multitude of church friends; then
rode into the morning.

We were following a dream but also representing the Oregon Trail Association. We carried greetings from the Association to the cities where the Trail ran. We were to tell them also
of our Oregon Centennial Celebration.

The first stop of the long ride was to Wascopam, the City of
the Flat Stones — Fort Dalles, where the Trail branched in the

early day. It was with real anticipation that we started on this lap of the journey which would take us across half the continent. The Dalles, gateway to the Inland Empire, is an attractive and historic city. One should see it first from the top of Seven Mile Hill west of town. From there it flashes scintillatingly on the granite strand of the mighty Columbia. We had ridden over the old Barlow Road the year before and had then come into The Dalles from Five Mile Creek.

We were now on one of the trails of the early emigrants from Wascopam to the Willamette Valley. Of course, they traveled it by boat and we were traveling it on our horses. Sometimes the road would run near the water and again high on the bluffs overlooking the river, but it was always filled with interest.

We were hunting the past and living in its spirit. As we rode, it became a present, fascinating fact. Very real to us was the group of log buildings there in the grove of white oak and yellow pine, the buildings of the Methodist Mission erected by Daniel Lee and H. K. W. Perkins in 1838 and called Wascopam. Like the builders they have long since turned to dust. Nevertheless there they were as real in our mind's eye as the Mission bell, used to call the red man to worship, which we would find among the relics of the fort.

Who can look at the old Mission bell and not picture the group of heathen worshippers who were called together by its mellow tones ringing out over river and rock and mountain heights? Who can fail to picture the childlike curiosity in their eyes, the naive wonder on their faces, as they tried to penetrate the mysteries of this strange new mode of worship.

Very real to us — and we could almost see her as we rode — was the coming of the golden-haired Narcissa Whitman to the Methodist Mission for companionship in the absence of her husband.

Also we could see the meeting and the parting here of two great missionary statesmen, Marcus Whitman, the Presbyterian, and Jason Lee, the Methodist. Lonesome hearts, real need, and true religion know no denominational lines. These two leaders knew each other. They respected each other. They met here at Wascopam in 1843. Here they held a series of conferences concerning the larger work of the Kingdom. Here

they clasped hands on an October day and parted never to meet
again.

Very real to us was the scene flashing before the mind's eye of
John Charles Fremont, as on November 25, 1843, in a flurry
of snow, he gave the order for his pack train of over a hundred animals, his little army of some twenty-five men,
and his Indian guides, to fall in and move forward on that second
exploring journey which would take him through the mountains
and far to the south.

We thought of Colonel Cornelius Gilliam and his five hundred volunteers resting here and waiting for supplies to be
brought up before advancing to the Whitman Mission, in the
Cayuse War in January, 1848. Very real indeed the burial
party and the firing squad and the taps sounding over the graves
of two of his men killed here while standing guard.

We had a vision of Lewis and Clark and their men as we rode
by the place at the foot of Liberty Street where they had
camped for three days, October 25, 26, and 27, as they came
down the great river in 1805 and again on their return in 1806.
It is said they called the little creek on which they camped,
Quennett, the Indian name for salmon trout, and the site of
Rock Fort Camp. Now an unfinished monument marks the
place of that camp.

Below The Dalles about twelve miles we saw Memaloose
Island, the place where Indians placed their dead. Just back of
the island, up the hill a piece, we saw the Balch cemetery, where
is buried that author-preacher, Frederick Homer Balch, whose
Bridge of the Gods is regarded by some as the greatest novel
ever to come out of the Northwest.

Though much of the past of The Dalles can be built up out of
pure thought and instructed imagination, as all of history and
historical events must be, there are things here, real things of
yesterday. There is Jason Lee's Pulpit Rock, where Jason Lee
and other early missionaries preached to the Indians in 1837.
In a shed attached to the historical society's building are wagons
and stage coaches of the early days. On the sandstone cliff above
the place of the fort it is said that one can find the name of U. S.
Grant etched by his own hand. The museum itself was the Sur-
geon's quarters. and is the only building left of the original
structures erected as part of the old fort.

If anyone had asked us why we were riding thus with two saddle horses and a pack animal, which carried our home for four and a half months on its back, and were not going on the usual way, smooth and swift on modern wheels, and if they had asked us what we expected to find, our answer would have been, "We are hunting the America of yesterday."

We rode into the morning at ten o'clock, the very hour and upon the very minute planned. We left the broad highway just before coming to the long, winding section that leads down around the Vista House. We took off on the Larch Mountain Road, to its junction with the Brower Road and down the rather steep and rough way over the side of the cliff to the lower level and camped that night some miles beyond Bridal Veil Falls.

The way down was somewhat rough and steep. Mrs. Beard, wishing to favor Black Fairy, walked the last mile. I guess I was too tired or just too plumb lazy to walk; I stayed on the back of Black Dynamite to the day's end.

Reaching the pavement, we crossed over, and finding a grassy tract, went into camp for the first night. We found in the morning that we had camped right in the middle of the very first road that had ever been followed through the gorge. We were very happy in this accidental choice of our first camp, for there was plenty of grass for the horses and fuel and water for our own needs. We were fortunate to be on our way at this time, for we seemed to be following the year into spring, the season when grass and water were most abundant. These two things are necessary to the party who would travel far with saddles in this mechanized day.

In the very center of the grassy tract we said, "Whoa." We were at home. Wherever night overtook us, for four and a half months, this word announced that we were at home again for another night. As usual, our first care was to unload the pack horse and stake her out on the picket rope, unsaddle Old Dynamite, putting his saddle on the pack saddle, then the Black Fairy, putting her saddle on top of the pile. This saddle carried saddle bags, in which were toilet articles — a shaving-set for the master, lip stick, powder and all for the mistress — and must be get-at-able. Such things are indispensable on any trip, especially so on a camping trip.

The only theology I remember from all the years in school was that a young minister should pray without ceasing and shave every day. And a little powder and a wee bit of lip stick goes along well with blue Levis and tan cowboy hat on even the loveliest of women.

Upon the saddles stacked in a neat mound were piled the blankets and chaps and bridles, all covered with a rubber poncho tied down with a long packing rope. The riding gear was thus protected from the hardest rains that might come. Weather permitting, the saddle blankets were always spread out to air and dry until bedtime.

The horses were soon picketed and contentedly grazing. The tent was lifted from the panniers and spread out upon the ground. Four long iron pins, one at each corner, were driven full length into the earth (a tent needs to be well anchored against wind and storm). The jointed, aluminum center rod was slipped through the door and erected and our house for the night was prepared. Homey it was, snow white and with a bright red top cap. With it pitched on a somewhat elevated mound, we were ready for rain, hail, snow or whatever the fates might decree.

A little hole about twelve inches square and six inches deep was scraped out for the fire. Over this the wire grill was placed, the coffee pot was superimposed, and our first dinner, or shall we call it supper, was on the way. The smaller the fire, the better for cooking, we found to be the right formula for camping.

While the better half of the team was boiling the coffee and frying the bacon, the other half was inflating the air mattresses, smoothing out the down sleeping bags and placing the panniers on each side of the tent door, the position they would occupy throughout the entire journey. System is very helpful in any mode of living; it is essential when travel-camping. In short, he was getting all things snug and shipshape for the night.

Mrs. Beard had sounded the call, "Come and get it," and we had just started the evening meal when there was a great commotion among the horses, the sickening sound of hoofs smashing against flesh. They were fighting. They were picketed too closely together. However, they had not broken any limbs and, with a few lashes with the lariat, the riot was subdued. When the battle was over we found that Black Diamond, the

READY FOR THE RIDE

EMIGRANT SPRINGS, EAST OF MOUNT HOOD

EAST TOLL GATE ON BARLOW ROAD

pack animal, had bitten Black Fairy just over the kidneys, making a sore that gave us trouble throughout the trip. The pack animal was separated from the other two horses and we returned to enjoy our dinner. But again, before the evening was over, Old Pack had rolled on a sharp rock and had torn a great hole over her withers; this also was to add to our concern for many a day. We had already experienced some of the trying things that must often have plagued the early pioneers.

Thanks to our many years in camping, our tent had a waterproof flour cloth sewed in and a bobbinet front and zippered over the door, shutting out all insects and we had learned to pitch it on elevated ground. It was well that we had made such preparation, for on many a night of the journey the flies and gnats and mosquitoes were terrible, almost driving the horses frantic, and, but for the insect-proof tent, we ourselves would have found life almost unlivable.

On this first night it rained, as it did night after night all summer long, but we were as comfortable and dry as two bears in a hollow tree and just loved to lie there all dry and warm and listen to the raindrops playing a slumber song on the tight drawn canvas.

Next morning we were awake at four o'clock and up at five, preparing to be on the move. Just as I put my head out of the tent door, the horses welcomed us with a friendly neigh. They wanted their oats. Such a call from his horses is music to the horseman's ear. When he hears it he knows they are in good health, good spirits, and ready to go.

As we lay waiting for daylight , we became aware of the wonder working mystery of spring. Just before the tent stood a wild current bush, now red with early blossoms. The rain had hung string after string of the purest pearls around it. Before it a hummingbird was vibrating on gauzy wings. Beyond it, on the higher ground, a tender new green had come to all the growing things, while the moss-covered sides and summit of the hills looked as if some giant had overturned upon them a great bucket of frost.

For five days we rode through the Columbia Gorge to Hood River, then for two days above it before we came to Wascopam. Many times we had driven through this gorge, past the multitude of lacy falls that tumble down the face of the cliffs, but we had really never seen it before. We did not care to hurry. When we came to an attractive spot or to a splendid scene, there we paused and looked and dreamed. For a time, at least, we were just lotus eaters, and the lotus eater's song could well have been our own, "We have had enough of action and of motion we."

Turning aside at Hood River, near which we had passed the Sabbath Day, we sought for a camping spot at the home of a true son and daughter of pioneers, Ed and Mable Lage.

There was no pitching of a tent this night, no staking the horses out for grass. The animals were put in roomy stalls in a big red barn, where they stood ankle deep in good dry straw. There, all dry and warm, they ate their full measure of sweet new oats taken from the host's well-filled bin. No wonder they were filled with life and action and wilful caprice next morning, and without tiring would carry us up and down the hills all day.

That night as we sat in the spacious drawing room of the ranch house we saw the setting sun give one last, long, lingering touch of his brush to Mt. Adams and Mt. Hood, turning them into fairy castles all made of gold.

That night we sat before the apple-wood fire in the great fireplace and listened to the stories of the pioneers that had been handed down through the years.

There was one story which was most informative, most fascinating, most gripping, a story of one of the real heroines of the trail. It was of a young Southern bride who came out over the trail in the earliest period of the covered wagons. This child had known only the tenderest care. She had been looked after and waited upon by servants and had not known even the labor of combing her hair and lacing up of her shoes. She was now a beautiful bride with the vision of her new home in the West. As the wagon was forded or ferried across the Platte River, her first child was born. The little newcomer weighed only two pounds and for three weeks was swathed only in cotton batting. Truly a wee bit of humanity to be lulled to sleep through the days and nights in such a cradle — the great, rough, rumbling conestoga wagon — but she came through well and strong and grew to make glad the little log cabin home in the Willamette Valley.

The happy couple laughed, they sang and labored together building their home. Then came '49, the year of the California gold rush. The fever of wealth to be found in the digging spread to the Oregon valley and into the log cabin of these two. The young husband took his pack, his gold pan, and supplies, and was away to the mines. The young bride and mother was left alone to carry on until his return. Scarcely had the footsteps of the young husband died away down the trail when a painted Indian came to the cabin door and, demanding food, pushed inside. He informed the frightened woman that her husband had gone away and would never return, and that she was now to be his squaw. He lay down upon the bed and ordered her to prepare him food.

"All right," she said, starting the fire in the fireplace, putting on the kettle of water to boil, shoving the iron poker into the flames, and ostensibly proceeding to prepare the required food, but when the water had reached the boiling point, she seized the dipper and thoroughly drenched the half-sleeping savage with the scalding liquid. Then beating him over the back and shoulders with the red-hot poker, she drove him screaming from the cabin.

Thenceforth, day after day, and night after night, the kettle was kept steaming and the iron heated. In a short stretch of weeks the husband returned. Soon after this the Indian came to visit the frontier home, saying to the husband, "Have um one brave squaw." And as the story is told, he became a true and lasting friend to the young couple, bringing them many gifts of venison and wild birds from the fields.

We were to hear many a story like this before we reached the end of our excursion into the past. Often long into the night we sat and listened and rejoiced in these romantic tales of the early days.

When we went out to the barn the following morning we found that the three horses had already been curried, fed, and prepared for the saddles. The panniers had not been unpacked for the night. Our packing chores were light.

The good nights's rest, with plenty of hay and oats, and now the rather chill, raw wind of the morning, made the horses nervous and high-spirited. Black Fairy seemed to be made of springs, Black Dynamite was ready to go indeed, but he did not want the heavy stock saddle on his back, so humped himself into a rainbow, when it was put on and cinched up. He reared up and pulled back every time I took the reins into my hands and grasped the pummel of the saddle. Finally, snapping a rope into a bridle, I led him up to a post, wrapped the rope around it, and, holding the loose end of the rope in my hands, proceeded to get on, Dynamite or no Dynamite.

When seated in the saddle I unsnapped the rope. We then had some lively seconds in adjusting our ideas. We finally settled the controversy on my own terms; at least, I was still in the saddle. He seemed to calm down and I reached out for the lariat with which I was to lead the pack, when the fun started all over again, now indulged in by Dynamite and the pack alike. There were some few more stiff-legged jumps and both horses came down hard and flat on the slippery road, falling into a tangle of reins, ropes, and panniers. My right elbow struck bed rock first, and for about a month the bruise was very painful, but we always ride with our reins in our left hand and we could fasten the pack's rope in a loop around the saddle horn. Thus organized, we got on the way.

It was great riding we had this day up over the Oregon Trail along the ridge of the hills. Before the day was over, we had passed through rain, hail, snow, and sleet. We had been held up by the carcass of a horse on a washed-out narrow part of the down hill road, and later by a big old turkey gobbler, which had his tail spread in the most approved turkey fashion and which waved his red, elephant-like probosis like a steamer in the wind. He sent the horses whirling around on their hind legs and plunging back up the trail. Time after time we tried to urge the horses past, but there he would stand always spreading that tail and issuing his challenge, and all three horses would turn again and run. Finally, we came back close to where the gobbler stood, stopped the horses, and waited. The old fellow meekly put down his tail and walked into the brush, and we rode on down the trail.

As the day wore on it became quite cold and disagreeable.

The wind seemed to increase and to find every opening or buttonhole in our riding garb. However, we put on our slickers, tied the scarfs about our necks, struck up a song, and plowed along till we came to the top of Seven Mile Hill. Here we met a rancher, Mr. George Johnson, and his wife Evelyn. Stopping him, we asked where along the way we might find water and grass and fuel for the evening camp. Turning, he pointed down the road and said, "Just go east down that road for a mile and a half and you'll find a ranch house on the right. The folks are not at home but camp there just the same and it will be O. K. If there is not grass to your liking, you will be able to get hay and oats at the house, I am sure. Well, I will be seeing you, good luck."

On he went, and down the hill we went.

Coming to the ranch house, we found a level spot on which we could pitch the tent, but, search as we might, by no stretch of the imagination could we find a patch of grass with enough on it to fit the needs of the horses. We decided to make the best of the situation and issue a double portion of oats to them and look for better things the next day.

We had scarcely pitched the tent and made camp for the night when a car came up, and from it the rancher we had talked with up the hill. He came to us and laughingly said, "Well, I see you found the way all right. Welcome to our home. In no case will you start a fire tonight. You are going to eat dinner with us, and spend the evening with us, chewing the rag." Then untying one of the horses, he said, "Shall we put them away for the night?" So here again we led the horses into a warm dry barn with plenty of clean, dry straw for a bed and wild hay as good as any horse's stomach could demand.

Dinner for us included good salt, home - cured bacon. It was not sliced too thin; it was just lean enough and salt enough with the smoke of the oak limbs, to be just right. On almost every day of the journey we had bacon, lean and fat, thick and thin, but never did we taste such bacon as this. It is doubtful if the emigrants on their trek westward ever had better though most of theirs perhaps had been home-cured.

And what fellowship was ours that night. All of life was our theme and field of talk. We heard and told the dreams we all had once held concerning life.

We did not hurry off in the morning, for we loved the fellowship of this ranch home and knew also that our journey would be one of only seven miles, and down hill.

We had now ridden both branches of the Old Oregon Trail from the Valley of the Willamette to The Dalles.

IV

CITY OF ECHOES

ECHO, OREGON, WAS OUR NEXT OB-jective. Walter Meacham of the Oregon Trail Association had said as he helped us mark out the way of our journey, "Echo is a very interesting town."

It is situated on the east bank of the Umatilla River. The very name of the river starts the echoes reverberating. This is the River *Euotalla* which the members of the Wilson Price Hunt party reached after their desperate trek across the continent. Here they found a friendly group of Indians and from them secured the food necessary to restore their spent strength. On its banks they rested until their spirits were fortified for the further journey down the Columbia to Astoria.

Near the confluence of this river with the Columbia, Crooks and John Day, who had been separated from the main body and given up as lost, were found starving and desperate and taken on down to Astoria.

Here at Echo or Brasfield, as it **was once called,** was situated the ferry run by Thomas Brasfield. Not far away, on the western bank of the Umatilla, had **been established Fort Hen-**rietta, a stout stockade for defence in the time of the Indian wars.

The very name of the town indicates the clash of opinions

held by individualists, which the pioneers assuredly were. Some wanted to call the place Henrietta, the name of the wife of an army officer. The fort had been named after her. But others were not like minded and wanted to call it Echo, the name of a daughter of one of the early settlers.

The new highway passes above it on the east. The first highway comes out to Pendleton on the old road along the river. It seems to lead you into another world, the world of yesterday.

As we entered Echo in the evening, we could almost hear the change of guard and the sound of the sunset gun from the log stockade, old Fort Henrietta, from across the swollen *Euotalla*.

Our start from Wascopam, The Dalles, was late in the day. We were in no hurry, however. We wanted to go to Celilo, the old fishing city of the Indians, and had to camp somewhere in the neighborhood. We settled ourselves early on the inviting green acres where, beyond Celilo, some government buildings are situated. This night we had superimposed a heavy miner's tent of eight-ounce canvass over the other one of balloon silk and, with a fire kindled just before the open door, no home in the city was ever more cozy.

Here we were soon visited by Mr. and Mrs. D. M. Coleman and their two children, Carol Sue and Bill. The Colemans who were in the government service, invited us to come to their home for dinner and stay with them over night. We accepted the first part of the invitation and had a great hour of fellowship and a bountiful dinner. However, we decided to sleep in our tent in order to be near the baggage and horses.

Just as we returned to the camp we were greatly surprised by a visit from a young couple we had married some five years before, Dean and Betty Taylor. They had brought along hot coffee and doughnuts and told us of their five years of happy married life.

As the night promised to be quite cold, we took the bright green blankets with white bands and put one on each horse. They looked proud and contented out there in the lush grass almost knee deep, wrapped up comfortably and warm.

When one's horses are well cared for the rider's mind and conscience are at rest.

At five we arose, looked out, and what a sight met our eyes! All three horses had rolled and got tangled up in the ropes and blankets. In place of wearing their bright green uniforms, they were covered with filthy, muddy rags. Old Dynamite and Diamond had ruined their blankets and Black Fairy had literally torn hers to shreds. Well, is was just too bad for their blankets would have afforded much warmth and comfort through many a cold night still to come and have been a real protection at times from the terrible insect pests.

We did not spend much time lamenting what had been done. We had learned a great lesson of life from an old Darky whose philosophy was , "Give up the unattainable and cooperate with the inevitable." We threw the blankets away, curried off the mud, saddled up, and at eight o'clock were on the way.

Just as we started a great freight train went by, puffing and groaning, and sending up circle after circle of black smoke that floated perfect rings for awhile, then dissolved into thin nothingness. True to a boyhood custom, we made a wish at every circle we saw and each was that the rain would cease and the days grow warm. We knew that our wishes were going to come true for all along the way, this day, the meadow larks sang their spring song, "Better wash your table cloth."

When we finally reached the plains of the Platte, one meadow lark would sing, "Better wash your tablecloth," and another would answer back, "Better keep your tablecloth clean." O. K., we said, and our little red and white checked table cover of oilcloth was washed meticulously every morning with soap and water.

Not long did we ride this day listening to the bird song until we too were singing.

This day we passed the Deschutes River where the men of the wagon trains drove out into the Columbia River to a bar, and so forded below the roaring rapids of the Deschutes. Then they climbed to the ridges of the hills above, and again moved over the high line to The Dalles. We did not attempt their way of crosssing this turbulent stream but were well content to pass over it on the modern bridge.

Riding along the shoulders of the concrete highway, we came to Biggs, the spot where the emigrants caught their first sight of the Columbia River. Here a marker records the fact.

You will travel far before you come to a more entrancing prospect. I will not attempt to describe the bronze hills, nor the mighty river, which has cut its way between them through the long centuries.

From the top of the gorge at Biggs the old way took off toward Wasco and then to the crossing of the John Day River.

It was with great thankfulness that we topped the crest and turned toward the place, for, as we started to leave the valley and go up Fulton Canyon, we had a serious incident that threatened to bring our adventure to a swift and sudden close.

At the turning of the way into Fulton Canyon Road we had stopped at a group of deserted buildings for rest and lunch. The rest had not calmed down the horses, which had been rather nervous and excited all morning, due to traffic. Several times all three had bolted and only alert riding and firm control had prevented them from running away. We had found it advisable always when mounting, for me to get seated firmly in the saddle on Dynamite, then for Mrs. Beard to hand me the rope of Diamond, then for her to mount Black Fairy. This we now did.

Because of a sore right arm, which prevented me from leading her, the pack animal's lead rope was attached to the horn of my saddle. But Black Fairy began to plunge, making useless all efforts for her rider to get into the saddle. I reached out to get the mare's reins, when Dynamite began to buck and Diamond started to do the same. Before I could get her rope freed from the saddle horn, she had passed around behind Dynamite, bringing her rope across my thighs, passed it under the Cheyenne roll, and pulled my saddle, with me in it, down on the side of my horse. I tried desperately to get Diamond's rope released from the saddle horn but found it impossible. I tried to reach my knife from a back pocket to cut the rope, but it, drawn tightly across the pocket, prevented me. The rope was beginning to cut deeply into my thigh and my grip on the reins with one hand and on the saddle horn with the other began to loosen.

It looked as though I was in for a pretty bad smash up when Mrs. Beard, at imminent peril to life and limb, managed to reach the head of Diamond and unsnap the lead rope.

With much difficulty I managed to get out of the saddle which was now under the belly of my horse and landed on my feet on the ground, with one hand still holding the reins. We were both pretty badly shaken. After resting a while, we thanked a kind providence for bringing us through, mounted and went on our way rejoicing.

We reached Wasco safely that evening where the road going south from the Columbia River cuts across the old emigrant trail near the Methodist Church. We camped in the park of the quaint little town. Here we meant to spend the Sabbath Day. We planned always to rest on the Sabbath. As one man said to us, "You rest on Sunday so the horses' shoes will not get too hot." Well, perhaps! The Lord's command for the Sabbath is still a good law on the trail or off.

After the morning church service we were taken out to Klondike by Mr. and Mrs. Leo Watkins. Yes, we found a Klondike here in Oregon. It's gold is the mountain of wheat mined from its vast farms and ranches. Here we found a big, general store with a post office. An old timer, A. B. Potter, entertained us with stories of the time when only the wild grass was growing where the wheat fields now yield their wealth, and cattle trails went where the broad highways now go. This pioneer graciously pointed out where the old trail had passed by, not a hundred yards away and directed us to where it crossed the John Day River. Rewarding indeed was that visit.

Early next morning we were on our way to the river crossing. Down through Grass Valley Canyon we went over a long, steep, rocky road, following the Stage Coach route, and came to the historic crossing beyond a shallow, sluggish creek.

Here we found a rather stately, weather-beaten ranch house set amidst a cluster of locust trees. This house had stood seventy-five or a hundred years through the development of the west. Here the early traveler had crossed the river. Here an old bridge had collapsed, carrying down a six mule team. It had never been rebuilt. Here we heard the story of two men who had been ruthlessly murdered nearby. Too, we were told the story of an old trapper who had been pursued by Indians, had eluded them in the tall sage brush, and then managed to stalk one of them. He told some friends about finding the Indian asleep and when he was asked what he did upon finding the slumbering savage he replied, "I just laid a smooth stone beside his head and came away." Some months later the Indian was found, and sure enough, the smooth stone was still lying beside his head. In fact, quite close beside his head.

As we came down the long, stony road to the river and up to the ranch house, we were greeted by an old gentleman, Mr. Merritt, who made his home with his son and wife, Mr. and Mrs. G. A. Merritt, the owners of the ranch. "Hi, there! Have you had dinner?" When informed that we had not yet had this mid-day blessing, he insisted that we come in and eat with the family. This we did and when the invitation was given to spend the rest of the day and night at this hospitable home, we gladly accepted.

The next day, Mr. Harry Allen, an old time cow-poke, would come to help us ford or swim our horses over the rising river. Mr. Allen had spent his life riding the range in this country and knew every hole and shallow of the river.

When we were preparing for our journey, we had been advised to stick to the highway until we came to Echo, as the bridge over the John Day at this crossing had been washed away, making necessary a detour of thirty or more miles either up or down the river.

Harry Allen duly came riding to the ranch the next day, mounted on his big, dappled gray. Horse and rider seemed as one. He looked over our outfit and voiced his approval of it all. Lovingly his hands passed over the hand-tooled saddles, and yearningly polished the silver-mounted spurs. We were proud of his approval.

At the crossing he led the way, then came Black Fairy, next Diamond (the Pack) and finally Old Dynamite. What a thrill it was to find the water getting higher and higher and feel the mighty strength of Old Dynamite as he smashed his breast against the wall of water. He had been a range horse, raised over in the Burns Country, so fording and swimming rivers was no new experience for him. The first few yards were thrilling indeed. I encouraged myself by saying, "Pho, there is nothing to this crossing of streams with livestock. The story of danger to the pioneers crossing rivers is just an exaggeration, a built-up legend to dramatize the past."

I laughed when the water touched my feet, but when it began to pour into the tops of my riding boots, the laughter suddenly died from my lips. Quickly my feet were lifted out of the stirrups, one leg was lifted and just as quickly the other was elevated and there I was — where, I suppose, every preacher should often be — on both knees, but perched high up on the Cheyenne roll and with one hand choking the saddle horn in order not to fall off in the fast-moving water. I was talking to myself and had just said, "If I get these horses out of this river, with no damage done, I will never take them into another river," — when the Dynamite began to come up out of the water onto the bank, and I finished my resolve with the words. "until I come to it." Well, we got safely over with no other damage done than two boots full of water and a wet pair of pants.

Reaching the shore, we moved up the very ruts cut deep by the wheels of countless wagons of the old migrants. The climb up the gulch was somewhat hard on the horses because of loose rocks slipping and rolling beneath their feet.

When we reached the plateau above we felt well repaid for the climb, for we came out upon a carpet of flowers. Keeping a lonesome looking butte on our right, we rode across this bloom-flecked highland and down into Rock Creek, then turned north over Shutler Flats to the Weatherford ranch. Here, again, we received a hearty Western greeting.

Before we left, the sores on the back of Diamond and Black Fairy had been skilfully cared for and doctored and the fetlocks of all three horses closely clipped. One of the owners of the ranch, Marion Weatherford, was a great lover of horses and liked to see them groomed to the last turn.

This large ranch is run by three brothers. The work is scientifically segregated and each brother has his own department to administer.

So great is the extent of this ranch that it is said a rider who had been lost for some days on the ranch came to the house one evening as a big tractor with its gang plows was coming in from a day's work. The rider of the horse asked the man on the tractor, "How big is this ranch, anyway?" The other replied, "Well, I can't just say, this is the first swath I have plowed. I started it the first day of April and I am just getting in tonight." It was then the last day of March of the following year.

Back of the founding of the ranch is a story of thrilling interest. The grandfather of the Weatherford boys was a man with an explorer's heart and the true pioneer spirit. He resolved to make the most of the countless opportunities offered beyond the Rockies. Oregon became to him a mighty obsession — a dream to be realized at any cost. He mobolized his every resource to make that dream come true.

He knew, of course, of the primitive conditions that would be encountered and was prepared for them. He knew that travel over the sod of the prairies would harden naked feet, but that for continuous labor on farm or ranch, shoes or boots would be badly needed, so he bought two pairs of heavy soled boots, put them in his wagon, and walked bare-footed on every mile of the way. As a result he was shod and ready for work when he arrived. The magnificent ranch is a monument to his dauntless courage.

After a hearty breakfast in the spacious dining room with the men of the ranch, Mrs. Beard eating with the mistress of the ranch in her private dining room, we were off over the hills through miles and miles of cultivated fields, then over a wide expanse of range land to Cecil, on Willow Creek.

Two or three miles from the big sheep ranch of John Krebs, we were met by two lovely young girls, Donna and Coleen Krebs, riding spirited horses, their curls flying in the wind. They were so free, so fair and laughingly full of life that they could well have been the very spirit of the spring. They had known we were coming and had come out to meet us lest we should get lost on the way, and to welcome us to their ranch home for the night.

We were met at the barn by the brother of the girls, Dick Krebs, who was soon telling us the story of sheep raising, of ranges here in Oregon, and ranges in Montana, of lambing, and wool clipping and watering and grazing. That night, in moving pictures, which he had taken, we followed the whole process from the lambing in the spring until the wool was shipped and turned into clothing, and the fattened mutton was hanging on the long, iron rails in the chilling rooms of packing plants. This lad had already found the thing that makes life worth living, something to do into which he could throw all his energy.

He showed us where the old trail had come down into the creek, near the barn where our horses were stabled. He said the way we were to take the next morning would be beside the trail at times and again right over the trail itself.

As we moved on next morning we passed an artesian well and a lonely cemetery. Here a stone marks the place where Colonel Cornelius Gilliam died in the Cayuse Wars. His body was put on a horse and brought to Dallas for burial.

Colonel Gilliam was a modern Cromwell, an ordained Baptist minister, who believed that one must pray but that there comes a time when real prayer is a grim, determined fight. He was in command of the Volunteer Regiment, raised by the Oregon Provisional Government, to fight the Cayuse War. Returning home from that campaign he was accidentally killed at Well Springs on March 24, 1848. It seems he was pulling a lariat from the wagon when it caught and discharged a rifle. The cleaning rod which had been left in the barrel was blown through his head, breaking off withing six inches of the penetrating point. Death was instantaneous.

Our way today was east by north. Late in the day we came to the end of the road and to a precipitous canyon, too steep for the horses to travel. We turned back west again for a mile. Then, looking far away to the north, we saw a lone rider moving toward the northeast. He did not see us and soon disappeared from view. We were just a little concerned and were not quite sure of the way, but turned our horses in the general direction in which the lone rider had gone. Traveling for about an hour and a half, we were gladdened to find a dim track going in this way. Getting on this, we followed it the rest of the afternoon. We had not gone far until it began to widen and deepen and it developed into a hard, beaten path, taking down into what we learned was Juniper Canyon.

At sundown, we came into a widening of the canyon where we found a level, grass-covered area, and at its edge the wagon of a sheep-herder. This looked good to us. We knew that as darkness came, so would come the herder to his wagon home, and that he would be glad to put us on our right way, in case we were not now upon it.

We pitched camp about two hundred yards away, staked out the horses, dug the usual pit for the campfire, cut up some stalks and roots of sagebrush, and began to prepare the evening meal. Suddenly, there was a commotion among our horses, then a shrill neigh. We looked up toward the east and saw a pure white horse standing like a great statue in the golden light of the setting sun. His head was lifted up, he appeared to be monarch of all he surveyed, making a formal reconnaissance of his domain. The three blacks answered his call and tried earnestly to get loose and go to him.

Fearful that he might get down among the horses in the night, I ran toward him, shouting, and he turned and with a few long, quick leaps disappeared over the hill and into the canyon. We saw him no more that night. The next day he followed us mile after mile, making our mounts restless and nervous. He left us only after we had passed through a line fence and had closed the wire gate behind us.

Coming back from our chase of the white stallion, we looked down the canyon to the north and there, creeping up over the whole canyon floor like a white frost, came the flock. We had reasoned well. Here they would gather about the home wagon, and here their master would come, and from him we would soon get the desired information.

We had just finished the evening meal when the herder came over to our camp. He carried a pail of water in one hand and some bacon and eggs in the other. He said, "I do not know who you are, whence you have come, nor where you are going, nor what you want, but I do know that anyone who has ridden this far down Juniper Canyon and intends to camp here for the night, needs water and may be in need of supplies."

I answered, "Well, Lad, we certainly do need some water but we are pretty well supplied with food."

"Well," he replied, "keep it all. The supply wagon will be in tomorrow with everything we need, and as you are not yet out of the canyon, you may need these things. I know my Boss would want me to see that any visitor passing by was well supplied."

That night, John Reynolds, for that was the name of the young Irish master of the flock, visited with us late into the night. I can see him now as I write these words. He would not sit down on some pieces of wood I had offered for a seat, but would kneel on one knee, holding his open hands to the fire, and shading his eyes from the glare of the flame. When he grew tired, he would change to the other knee.

He was a Roman Catholic lad and I was a Presbyterian-Catholic minister. When we parted the next morning, he came over to the camp with another pail of water, the last word he said to me was, "Chaplain, when you get back to your church, just say a little prayer for me."

I answered back as I rode away, "Lad, I will not wait until I get back to my church. I will be saying a little prayer for you every day of the journey."

When he went back to his wagon, after our long visit in the night, some of his dogs came and lay down beside our door. The whole flock of two thousand white-wooled sheep moved in close and bedded down. Any hour of the night I could have reached out on either side and put my hand on a gentle, wooly head.

Late in the night I went out to see if the horses were securely picketed. What a marvelous scene greeted my eyes! There they were, three black rocks standing in a sea of white. Over in the dim shadow of the hills in the west was the wagon of the herder. There was my own white miner's tent with its red cap. Over all the silvery moon rode in a cloudless sky. As the angels of the Lord long ago had gathered around Jacob's tent at Mahanaim so these white angels of this later day had gathered around ours.

We knew that all was well here in our tent home in Juniper Canyon. We went back into our tent and were soon lost in sweet and dreamless sleep.

Like ships that pass in the night and speak each other in

passing, we had met, we had spoken, and now we parted.

We parted in the way I have said, he to lead his tender flock down the canyon to the green pastures and the still waters, and we to take up the old trail again.

After long hours we came to a line fence, for which we had been looking, and were glad to find that our way led through it, for there was the gate we could pass through to close against the big white horse that followed us, causing us a great deal of trouble.

For half the day we rode steadily on, mostly toward the east, but sometimes turning north, then reached a place where we became seriously confused about directions. We had dismounted and had eaten our lunch of bacon sandwiches and canned tomatoes and were earnestly consulting the compass, the map, and our own judgment concerning the way. We were finding it downright difficult to make a decision, when over the hill we saw a horseman coming in our direction. We knew he was a range rider.His horse had the sure, long gait of the cow pony and he rode it as though he were a part of the saddle itself. He was a rather short man, light and spare of build. We asked him about the way, two of which he pointed out, one that was fairly easy to follow and which probably kept near the Old Trail, the other somewhat more difficult, as it had some hills and canyons to climb and cross, but was much nearer. We decided to take the first.

He asked us who we were, where we had come from, why we came, and where we were going, and if we had seen any cattle on the way. I was rather under the impression that he may have taken us for cattle rustlers. At least, with my tongue in my cheek, that is what I told Mrs Beard afterwards. He looked us over rather critically.

When he asked us where we were going and we told him to Independence,Missouri, where the Old Trail started, he said, in a rather sarcastic vein, "Well, that is a long, hard way, I know I could make it," and he emphasized the I, "But I don't think you can."

"Why, you little weazened-up shrimp," I thought, though I did not say so, (for I hate to hurt another man's feelings and then, too, he had really helped us out by giving us directions for finding the way), "you little weazened-up shrimp," and I was emphasizing every word in my own mind, "I could ride the very pants off you and only half try."

For the rest of the day the meadowlarks were singing their songs and the black birds were piping their love notes. We caught frequently the whir of a China pheasant cock. We watched the clouds drift like stray lambs across the vast, open Heaven. We heard and saw all these things, but always the words of that little weazened-up shrimp of a cow poke kept coming back and crowding things out of my consciousness, and I could hear him say, "Independence, Missouri, that is a long, hard way, I know that I could ride it, but I don't think you can." And I always answered back, "Why, you little shrimp, I can ride the very pants off you, and I know it."

When we came into Echo that night, like an echo out of the hills seemed to come his voice, "It is a long way to Independence, Missouri, I know I could ride it, but I don't think you can."

But We Did!

V

TREK TO HOUTAMA

The year truly was at the spring. And the spring was at morn when we set out for Houtama or Pendleton. It was April and we had now been on the road sixteen days. We said good-by to Doc Cunha, owner of the ranch, and to Mr. and Mrs. Ed Hall, his genial caretakers, where we had camped this night. They graciously invited us to linger longer but tonight we would be pitching camp at Houtama, or somewhere near it, for it was only twenty-four miles away. We were by this time pretty well hardened and twenty-five or thirty-five miles a day was not an especially hard journey any more.

We were both in the saddle and Mrs. Beard had just given the order to march, when we became aware of the unpleasant fact that Old Dynamite had cast a shoe. For a few minutes the very sunshine seemed to go out of the sky.

We had no shoes or nails or hammer. A shoeless horse could not travel far on the trail without going lame. We moved on across the bridge and into Echo and inquired if a farrier could be found. The man whom we asked replied that he didn't suppose that such a person still existed in the State, but that there was a good blacksmith in the town who could shoe horses, and pointed to his shop a little down the street. Well, we didn't stop to go into the meaning of names, for we thought that a man who could put a shoe on Dynamite would be just as welcome whether he was called a farrier or a blacksmith. So we proceeded to his shop. We found not only a blacksmith but a farrier and an artist. He was a man who knew not only his horseshoe nails and how to drive them home but he knew horse nature as well. He put that shoe on Old Dynamite without swear words or struggle and the old fellow seemed to like it and stepped proudly out on his new iron.

Now off, we once more found that the year was at the spring. Our way led along the bank of the Umatilla River. It too, like the John Day, was in flood from the heavy rains and was doing real damage to some of the farms through which it ran.

The road, however, was truly enchanting. The white-trunked cottonwoods were sending forth their leaves of tender green, making a line of finest lace around the breast of the copperish hills. Here were many flashes of red-winged blackbirds bursting their throats with the joy of spring. The whirring wings of China pheasants made sweet music for our ears, and clumsy, grotesque turtles slipping off their sunny logs into the yellow waters of the slough brought to our hearts a longing for the old swimming hole.

On the main trail just outside Pendleton, we were met by a delegation from the Chamber of Commerce, Mr. Oren Allison, secretary; Reverend Earl P. Cochran, of the First Presbyterian Church; Fred Savage, banker, who has charge of all historic displays connected with the Pendleton Round Up.

Our horses were taken to the Rodeo grounds, put in a barn, watered, fed and doctored. Our camp was pitched near the barn but it was made known, most emphatically, that though Pendleton was a Rodeo town and always had camps and camping places for its visiting Indians, that we must have the best room, the softest beds and the best food that Pendleton could furnish. So we were taken to the hotel as guests of the city.

Pendleton, or *Houtama,* as I love to call it, is a place noted for its hospitality. Every year vast crowds come to its Round Up and never go away dissatisfied.

This Round Up is probably the finest spectacle of the Old Days staged anywhere in the world. Here East truly meets West and every year the past is reborn.

Very interesting is the succession of names by which this western city has been known. We find them listed in *Oregon Geographic Names* by Lewis A. McArthur. A trading post was established by Dr. William McKay in 1851 near the mouth of McKay Creek. This post became known as *Houtama,* then as Marshall Station, then as Swift Station, then as Middleton and finally as Pendleton. It was the early center of a vast cattle empire, with all the romance and riot of the cow town. Even now, whenever the name Pendleton is mentioned, we think of Indians, cowboys and bucking horses, but also of a city set among bronze hills. It is hard to believe that the land on which Pendleton now stands was traded for a team of horses.

When the delegation met us, Dr. Cochran informed me that I was to fill the pulpit and preach in his church on the Sabbath.

"O. K.," I said, "but I left my gown behind and will have to come to you just as I am in the togs of the trail."

"That will be all right," he agreed.

It was a service of beauty and dignity. I was somewhat nervous appearing in a red woolen shirt, blue jeans, and high-heeled cowboy boots, with pants legs tucked in the tops, and would have been more nervous had I known what was going to happen. But being entirely oblivious of the coming event, I arose and started to offer the meditations of the day, when someone shouted out in full toned voice, "Powder River." Suddenly, all nervousness left me. I was at home. I was among my own kind here in this western town. I was with my friends and welcomed by a comrade of the Old Brigade. It was the Battle Cry of the Wild West Division, the 91st., that had played such a stirring part in the First World War. Often had I heard it at St. Mihiel, in the Argonne Woods, in Belgium. "Powder River," was the cry, "Let 'er buck" was the answer.

When we later went down to the Rodeo grounds for the horses, we met Nolan Skiff, editor of the *East Oregonian*, and Buz Howdyshell, the photographer. The latter gave us a good laugh and a hearty welcome. He had wanted to get some pictures of our outfit, mounted and ready for the trail, with mountains and cloud effects and other things, which only a photographer knows, and complained to us that he could not take a picture with clouds if there were no clouds in the sky.

Well, we were glad there were none right then, though we had met up with rain, hail, or snow in some part of almost every day since leaving Portland on the first of April.

On Sunday we attended the installation of Reverend T. Samuel Lee, a young Korean, as Presbyterian minister, over the congregation of the Tutuilla Mission. Here we had a delightful evening. Jimmie Cornelison, a personal friend, here for the installation, had served this Mission for years, being greatly beloved by the Indian congregation. We heard some fine singing by the Indian choir. In the choir we saw a beautiful Indian girl. Looking at her, we could readily see why so many of the trappers and Mountain Men of the early day took Indian girls for their wives.

Dr. Cochran, a fine horseman, rode with us out of the city and put us on the trail hard by Tutuilla Mission. His spirited sorrel gelding was a fast walker, and the first seven miles were over almost before we realized it.

Our way passed by the Herb Thompson Ranch and up over a cattle driveway toward Cabbage Hill. As we left the ranch we ran into some men rounding up horses. One of them was a tough - looking customer, abusive to the exhausted horse which he was riding. We were very happy when he disappeared over a neighboring hill.

As we were climbing the rather soft and laborious path up the mountain-side, we noticed a sheep dog was keeping parallel with us but about three hundred yards away. He followed us all afternoon and came into camp that night. We tried our best to send him back, but it was useless. The next morning his master found him and took him home. Dogs and horses seemed to have a desire to follow us, but we did not like to collect them in this way.

This day we had some trouble with the pack animal. Coming to an irrigation ditch, we paused to let the horses drink. When the Pack had filled her stomach, she suddenly desired to wet her back. So she lay down and tried to roll over and over in the deep water of the ditch. This we found she would try to do at every ditch, creek, river, or pond we came to, so we had to take measures accordingly. We kept the rope fastened to my saddle horn, and at the first, slight bending of her knees, would swing Old Dynamite around. Off he would go, pulling the stubborn, protesting Pack with him. We got rather used to this habit of hers, and after we found that it was almost impossible for water to penetrate the closely packed and hooded panniers, we did not mind it much if she were quicker on the trigger than we were and got down and rolled before we could interfere.

Thursday we met up with one of the strange tragedies of nature. Riding along the trail, we saw a startled China pheasant cock rise swiftly out of the grass, and flash across in front of the horses and dash itself against the single strand of wire stretched along the fence beyond. A few inches higher or a few inches lower and he would have been safe in his flight, but here he was just a handful of golden splendor from which life had sped. Strange is this thing we call fate.

We camped at Emigrant Springs Park under a great tree. The horses were tied out to three other trees in the scattered grove. How clear and cold and delicious the water from the springs. How good to think that many a tired, weary man or woman or boy or girl had paused here to be refreshed, and had gone on restored and rejoicing. This spring was probably discovered by Jason Lee in 1834.

Emigrant Pass reaches a height of some 3800 feet, and it was quite cold at night. Frost lay all about us, and water was frozen in the bucket, but we were warm and sleep was dreamless. These down sleeping bags, secured from the Army Surplus, are just the thing. The minute one crawls into the bag, he becomes warm. They are also very light and easy to pack and carry.

As we arose the next morning, we were thrilled to look off toward the east and the south and see the day coming over the white grandeur of the Blue Mountains. Cruel and heartless things are mountains when one violates their laws, but sublime, inspiring havens of safety to one who knows and keeps their laws. As we looked at these faraway hills, we felt a mighty longing to be moving toward them, to be entering and losing ourselves in their luring massiveness. How happy the early emigrant had been to get out of them, to leave them behind, to come out on the top of the Pass and to look over the plateau and rolling hills where Pendleton now stands.

It was now the twentieth day of April, a day we were to pass in pure, I almost said, sheer animal enjoyment. Perhaps purely spiritual enjoyment would be a better description. Our early hours, of course, were spent in passing through this Emigrant Springs Park. We heard now the first frogs of spring. How homey is their call. The meadowlarks were singing for us on every mile of the ride. We saw where a beaver had cut down a tree along the banks of a creek. For our noonday lunch we had cold water, dry white bread, and a delicious apple. No banquet hall ever had food that tasted better.

We passed through Meacham, which rather boasts that, for a day, it was the Capital of this great nation. That was when President Harding was there dedicating a marker to the old pioneers. Several markers at Meacham remind us of these old pioneer days and bring back their thrilling history. Here ran the Stage Coach Line. Here they were often raced and stopped and robbed by the highwaymen. Jason Lee preached a sermon here. Dead Man's Pass marks a battle fought with the Indians near Meacham in 1878. Near here lies buried the child born to Madam Dorian of the Overland Astorians in December, 1811.

We found it difficult to select a camping spot for the night.

The canyon is narrow and we had ridden twenty-six miles before we came to a place with area enough to make our camp, but after we had passed the Ezra Meeker Springs we arrived at a place at the side and below the road with room enough for the tent. Beyond this and in a creek bottom were water and grass for the horses. Very near the camp we found some brush for the fire. So we said our usual, "Whoa," and we were at home.

It was clear and cold that night, so cold that we must break ice in the bucket the next morning, and so clear that the moon above threw a great light through the white cloth of the tent. We found it hard to sleep, as our thoughts were teeming with the thrilling stories we had heard of galloping horses, creaking stage coaches, masked bandits, lurking Indians, and sudden death along this stretch of the way.

Next day it was still clear and cold and somewhat windy. So we built our morning fire in front of the open door of the tent and ate breakfast inside. Without moving an inch, we could reach the coffee pot, help ourselves to its delicious contents, and then place it back on the grill to warm up. The sizzling hot bacon and eggs made us hungry as wolves. The heat of the fire coming through the open door made us so comfortable that we were tempted to call it a day, even before we started, and surrender ourselves to idleness and animal enjoyment. Then we remembered that Independence, Missouri, was still a long way off and we would have to keep moving if we ever reached it. So we conquered our desire for ease and got moving. We planned to camp that night at La Grande, and the next night at the Hugh Snider Ranch some ten or twelve miles beyond.

Soon after starting we came to the highway and to a long, narrow bridge which was something of a hazard on account of traffic, but the State Police solved the difficulty for us. They flagged down the traffic at each end of the bridge until we could hasten over. Whenever and wherever we were compelled to come out on the highway, we found the State Police cordially concerned for our safety, often directing us to places where we could find comfortable camping quarters.

While having an argument with Dynamite and the Pack, a

sudden gust of wind blew my hat off and I rescued it at the very edge of the Grande Ronde River. With hat pulled down tightly on my head, we resumed the argument with the horses, the argument ending in my favor.

La Grande is well named, grand in its situation of beauty on the rim of the Grande Ronde Valley, lying between the Blue Mountains and the Wallowas; grand in its history, having been for nigh on to a quarter of a century a camping place for the wagon trains. Later it was a mining town, and today is a lively industrial town of the West, grand in its people. We were given hearty welcome by representatives of the Chamber of Commerce. Our camp was pitched on the green lawn of the radio station, K.L.B.M., whence out over the air goes the "Voice of the Blue Mountains." Here we met and heard the master violinist, Rubinoff, who signed and gave us a souvenir.

Black Fairy proved herself a true descendent of Morgan Ley Fey by lying down three times and trying to roll off her saddle before we could get the Pack unloaded. Just before the sun went down, a robin came and perched in a tree and sang for us our slumber song and the rain that poured down all night long did its share to make rest and sleep under canvas a delicious experience.

Next morning on our way out to the Diamond One Ranch, we were met again by Mrs. Hugh Snider, its mistress, on a fiery Arabian mount. It was a pleasure to see her ride this spirited horse and it was delightful entertainment we found in her ranch home.

On our way out we passed the historic Ezra Meeker Spring which should be set aside for public use. We also passed a farm where an old German long ago had tried to set out and raise one of every kind of tree that grows in the world. But like so many of our dreams, his dream had vanished with the years. He has gone, the trees have gone, but the memory of a really great dream still lingers in the Grande Ronde Valley.

Well, many dreams prosper or turn to ashes, but God Himself had a dream here and He fixed it in the rocks that forever endure. He made here some chains of mighty mountains and then fastened them together with a gorgeous jewel which men have called the Grande Ronde Valley.

South of the Diamond One Ranch we saw where the Old Oregon Trail came down over the hills. We saw also the earlier trail down which Marcus Whitman and his bride and the Spaldings descended to the level floor of the valley.

That night, after a happy party with the La Grande Riding Club, the old days were made to live again for us from the lore of the valley and the stories from the hills which the enthusiastic mistress of the ranch had collected through the years. We were very much interested in the legend of gold buried up in the hills. We heard many stories of the kind as we traveled east. And we found many a place where men had actually dug in the earth to find the buried gold. In this case a burro, a man and a bag of gold had all been buried together.

Out of the Grande Ronde Valley, we struck up through Ladd Canyon for North Powder and then for Baker. The Old Trail probably went up this canyon or along the crest above it. We knew that the old Stage Coach Road went up here. At the crest of the climb we had to dismount and readjust the Pack and had a hard fight to get back on Old Dynamite. I almost said to get back on the Black Devil, for devilish he certainly was that day. He seemed to be affected by the weather.

It was a blustery and stormy day through which we rode. Rain, hail, snow and sleet came marching and counter-marching in regular battalions. We passed through several cattle-guards and each one was the scene of a battle with the big black horse. At every guard we must dismount, pass through, close the gate behind, and then get up on the horse who was always ready to veto such mounting.

At times we were almost numbed with the chill of the day. We put on sweaters and leather coats and then tucked our long, flowing scarfs around our necks We even tried walking and leading the horses, but this was just too big and complicated a job. Once, while walking, Old Dynamite actually stepped on one of my spurs, throwing me violently to the ground, but he had the decency to shy aside and did not walk all over me. Stopping now, with the persuasion that it was better to freeze to death riding than to be stamped to death walking, we got back again into the saddles. Riding through the storm, we began to appreciate what must have been the terror of the early travelers through the mountains in the winter season.

Just at this time, the words of the little, weazened-up cow poke (who had opined that he knew he could ride the long trail but did not think I could), came to me, and again the answer that I silently made, "why you little shrimp, I'll bet my big, double-bladed jack-knife that I can ride the very pants off you." This challenge seemed to warm us both, for I told Mrs. Beard about it, and, beginning to laugh, we touched up the horses a little and rode into North Powder, once a Stage Station on the Old Trail. Here we got hot coffee and a lunch and, thus warmed inside and out and refreshed in mind and rehardened in spirit, and told, moreover, by a State Police-man we were expected soon in Baker, we rode happily on into what now began to look like a real adventure.

I had married the mother and father of this State Police-man some twenty-three years before and had lost all track of the family since. On this journey we were to find many an old friend and many a war buddy whom we had not seen for years.

We camped for the night at Haines. Some miles out of town, we had ridden up to a ranch home, hoping to turn the horses into its pasture and camp near the house where we would find water, but I guess we looked too tough, for no one would come to the door to answer our knock, though we had seen some one enter and could hear people inside. So we rode into the town and then found a comfortable barn and feed for the horses. When we left Haines for Baker, a young fellow offered the use of his truck to save the horses and us a long hard ride. But we knew that had the emigrants not been tough-souled men and women as well as strong in body and resolute in purpose, they never would have made the journey. If the going was get-ting hard and at times very tiresome for us, how much more so it must have been for them who could drive their oxen and wagons not more than twelve or fifteen miles a day, while we could make from twenty to thirty on our good, strong horses. It is true that at the end of some days riding we would be desperately weary, but the smell of frying bacon and the odor of good, strong coffee, mingled with the pungent fragrance of the smoke from the wood fire, would soon set us right and we would decide that the rewards had been well worth the ride.

Every morning we would arise and be on our way with a fresh, childlike expectancy. We would be eagerly wondering what the day's travel would bring forth. We were indeed riding into the morning, we were renewing our youth. We especially felt this the morning we rode from Haines to Baker.

The blackbirds were a riot of color. In every pond or meadow we found wild ducks swimming. The snow-clad Elkhorn Range was a path of glory, fit only for angel's feet to tread. True the wind would sweep down from the mountain tops at times with such power it would reach the very marrow of our bones, but our blood seemed to be running with the speed and warmth of youth and we did not mind.

Just outside Baker we were met by Dr. Sydney Walker, the Presbyterian minister, and by a delegation from the Chamber of Commerce and by many riders from the Oregon Trail Riders Club — Mrs. E. B. Moeller, president; Miss Catherine Tyler secretary; Mrs. Ted White; Miss Etha Langrell, board director; and Mr. P. M. McAllister, past president. Other women of the club came out in cars and with thermos bottles of strong, hot coffee.

Along with the coffee, Mrs. Ed Moeller presented us with a complimentary membership card in that fine organization. Again our horses were put under skilled care, and we were escorted to Baker's finest hotel and lodged in its best suite. In vain we protested that we were riding the Old Trail, and that camping out under all situations was one of the experiences we wanted to try. We were informed that we would find plenty of opportunities for all these things. And we most assuredly did.

Baker was just off the Old Trail, but we went out some four or five miles east to the markers. Here we could see the old ruts where the trail came around the hills and went on down to the Missouri Flats. Here we were told of the Lone Pine tree, which used to stand in the plains, and toward which the travelers used to steer as the mariner steers by the north star and at which many a wagon train had been wont to stay. The tree had long since disappeared, cut down by some thoughtless person perhaps, but its memory still lingers, and its story will long be told.

At Baker we were once more made aware of what a small place the world is and how quickly time flies. At the close of the morning service in the Presbyterian Church, a comely matron, Mrs. Eunice Hunt Muray, took my hand and said, "Chaplain Beard, you will not remember me."

"Why not, Eunice," I replied, "you were one of my pets in the church at Hoquiam, Washington. You were a very wee and a very pretty lassie when I first lifted you to the platform to practice a Christmas play in 1910."

I had not seen her for some twenty-five years. That night we visited her cousin Roy Hunt's ranch, where she was visiting. There we tasted moose meat for the first time in our lives. We thought it quite fitting to be eating wild game on our trek over the Old Trail, even though the moose had been killed in Canada.

After a Sabbath of delicious rest and delightful fellowship, we left in a flurry of snow. This continued intermittently all day and we were well chilled and were quite ready to call it a day and turn into camp when, passing by a ranch house, early in the evening, the voice of Mrs. Earl Bowman, joint owner with her husband, called hospitably to us from the gate, "Haven't you ridden about far enough for the day? We have been waiting and watching for you; you look tired. Chaplain Beard, put the horses in the barn. You will find plenty of hay and grain for them, and supper is about ready."

Now, who could have refused an invitation like that?

What a delightful evening was spent in that old ranch house, hearing tales of the early days and of things as they used to be. It had stood beside the trail for better than seventy-five years, in fact, for almost a hundred years. It was surrounded by a border of great elm trees, of about the same age as the house, brought out from Iowa.

Next morning, after mixing some lamp-black with kerosene to make a thick paste and covering the sores of the Black Fairy and the Pack with this old cowboy remedy for saddle sores, we took off for Dixie, about twenty-five miles away. The day was cold and blustery, and the horses were hard to manage. The intermittent blasts of snow-filled wind turned at times into a blizzard and it was with real joy we caught sight of a three-cornered bit of meadow, fenced in by a great cliff and the highway. Water was very handy, and there was plenty of wood. We turned in, disposed of the horses for the night, and had started to make the fire to prepare supper, when a lad who had been in the C.M.T.C. with me in Vancouver, Washington, years ago, Dale Phillips, came down to the camp, saluted as in the old days and said, "Sir, I have the honor to inform you that dinner is ready and waiting just a few miles down the road. I am going to get you there and get you back. Everything will be O. K. in camp, I am sure. Come on, things are reversed now. This is a command."

At his mother's home at Lime we sat down to a dinner of T-bone steaks, the like of which I have not seen since the war. I wonder if any buffalo ribs or steak of venison ever tasted better to hungry travelers across the plains than these did?

When we started for the Farewell Bend in the Snake River next morning we knew we were in for a good day. Golden sunshine had flooded the peak of the great mountain just west of the camp and had begun to flow down its sides to mingle with the gold of the river. We had thrown open the door of the tent and washed our hands, our eyes and our very hearts and souls with its warm, life-giving stream. It was not at all hard to get up this day and it was not hard to travel.

We started the day with a song, "O day of rest and gladness, O day of joy and light." The song was interrupted by the horses plunging and careening as we tried to pass under the clanking, shrieking baskets of the aerial cable-line that were tearing out the very bowels of the mountain at Lime. The bloated body of a drowned steer, carried along by the swollen waters of the river, took the very words of the song momentarily from our lips. However, the day was just too fine for anything to spoil. We passed through Huntington, in a canyon of the Burnt Mountains, half asleep in its noon-time rest. Along this trail Wilson Price Hunt and his Overland Astorians had dragged their weary feet on their way to the Columbia River and Astoria. We passed by the bowl in the hills alongside the road where a party of emigrants had been massacred. We reached Farewell Bend, where the Old Oregon Trail leaves the Snake and strikes out northwest to the Burnt River, still singing the sweet old hymn, "O day of rest and gladness."

We stopped at the very edge of the Snake River. We pitched camp and cut the wood for the evening fire, swinging the axe, as we persuaded ourselves, in true pioneer fashion.

We kept repeating what we had found on the markers, "The Wilson Price Hunt Party, after its terrible, haunting experience along the canyons of the Snake, were reunited here. Bonneville camped here. Fremont camped here," and here we will camp. We who ride back over the way they came will have good company tonight. We will be surrounded by the heroes of the faith. We took a good, cold plunge in the Snake and retired, persuaded that we had enjoyed as wonderful a spring day as man had ever known. Gradually the honking of the geese in the river died away. All the world was still.

How quickly the face of nature can change. Yesterday had been so warm, so genial, so full of sheer animal comfort that it seemed those things must last forever, but when we started for Ontario and the Idaho border, we took off in a cold, drizzly rain which was soon whipped into a howling storm of sleet and snow. Needing a little stimulus to our drooping spirits, we composed a little song and began to sing it as we rode along,

> *The rain will cease to fall, my Dear,*
> *The sun will soon break through,*
> *The clouds will roll away, my Dear,*
> *The skies will turn to blue,*
> *As we ride down the "Long Trail Together."*
>
> *The hours fly by on golden wings*
> *The miles, they speed by too,*
> *In happy hearts a love song sings*
> *For ours is tried and true,*
> *And we ride down the "Long Trail Together."*
>
> *Before our tent the fire will gleam,*
> *Bright stars will light the sky,*

While calm above with silver beam,
The guarding moon sails high,
For we ride down the "Long Trail Together."

Soon journey's end will come, my Dear,
The long ride then be through,
The lights of home will shine, my Dear,
Home lights for me and you,
Who ride down the "Long Trail Together."

The horses, and especially Old Dynamite, seemed to enjoy the singing, and would swing along in perfect time. Horses are not so dumb. We found that we had based the theme of the song on the facts of nature, for by the time we had reached Ontario, the sun was out and it was springtime again in Oregon.

On the way in we had a very narrow escape from being run down by a big truck and on the way we made a recorded interview while in the saddle, and next night listened to it, as it was sent out on the air by the radio station at Weiser. We are very sure the old covered-wagon travelers would not have thought such a thing possible.

At Ontario we were located in the Fair Grounds. Here a skilled veterinarian, Dr. L. M. Koger, cared for the sore-backed horses but would take no fee. Roy Brewer, a fine Irish horseman, cut the saddle blankets to relieve pressure upon the sores, then, with a new shoe for Black Fairy and a soft pad for her back, we continued our ride at eleven o'clock.

We reached Nyssa early in the afternoon and were met by Mr. Roy Holmes, of the Owyhee Riding Club, who put all three horses into his big truck and took us all out to the ranch of Mr. Neil G. Dimmick, drill master of the club, for a meeting of his organization, and brought us back to Nyssa the next morning. We did not saddle the horses nor put the panniers on the pack animal out at the ranch but waited until we returned to town. Out at the Rodeo Grounds, Mr. Dimmick helped us saddle up and get the kicking, bucking Pack loaded properly. Then he pointed in the general direction where Old Fort Boise once stood. With many a kindly good-by from the citizens of this fine town, we crossed the Snake into Idaho at 1:30 on May the first.

Not far from Nyssa, on the Boise River and near where Parma now stands, is the place where Tom McKay of the Hudson's Bay Company located Fort Boise in 1834. This was a

WAGON RUTS UP WINDLASS HILL FROM ASH HOLLOW,
NEBRASKA

DESCENDANTS OF THE SURVIVORS OF THE MASSACRE
NEAR OAK, NEBRASKA

COURT HOUSE, INDEPENDENCE, MISSOURI—THE END OF THE TRAIL

shrewd move in the relentless game being played at that time by the great fur trading companies for the control of the lucrative fur industry. McKay built this fort or station to checkmate Nathaniel J. Wyeth, even as Wyeth, in that same year, had already built Fort Hall, which he hoped would be as a great, immovable rock rolled into the garden of the Rocky Mountain Fur Company, whose officials had already double crossed him. In 1836-37, the fort was moved to its new location on the Snake River.

As we looked over the place where this second fort once stood, we were told by a rancher that, as late as 1906, some buildings of the original structure of the second fort were still standing. These walls had been made of adobe. The first fort near Parma, erected in 1834, had been built of cottonwood logs. Nothing now remains of either fort.

Wood rots; earth, though sun dried or kiln-burned, disintegrates, dissolves; but the pattern of life and of history planned by the Great Weaver lives on and surely takes form. He mingles with His fixed design even the plans, the loves and hates and selfish deeds of men. How well this thesis, which occupies our minds, was illustrated when we recalled the history of the three trading posts erected along the Old Trail in the year 1834 — Laramie, Hall, Boise. All were erected to further selfish interests but were all used by the Master Weaver to further the common good. All were erected at places which later proved to be strategic points for meeting the needs of the vast floods of emigration that flowed along this historic corridor of empire. All three became safety islands in a vast sea of weariness, hardship and danger. The story of Fremont, the Pathfinder, and of Whitman, the missionary, at this Fort Boise could have been told at Fort Laramie and at Fort Hall, of thousands that passed in their footsteps.

Fremont came here on October 8, 1843. He was cordially received and generously entertained, and when he was ready to cross the Snake on his renewed journey, and when his rubber boats were entirely inadequate for the task, the canoes always kept in readiness, were put at his disposal.

The Whitman Party arrived on August 19, 1836, rested for three days; feasted on the vegetables, enjoyed the fresh butter; washed their clothing; a duty dear to the heart of women; traded some of their worn-out cattle for others to be delivered at Walla Walla; held divine services; left behind the highly prized wagon; and took off for Walla Walla, rested in body, refreshed in mind and spirit, ready for the last, long march.

These very stories seemed to bring encouragement and renewed strength to us, as, with the direction reversed, we started back over the three-hundred-mile ride to the White Fort.

VI

WAY TO THE WHITE FORT

It stood, a thing of gleaming white, amid the green meadows, by the side of the silvery Snake. It was the heart's desire of the thousands of weary men and women who came across the plains in the days of the Great Migration. Often the burden of their talk, as they gathered around their campfires at night, had been this: "When we come to Fort Hall we can rest, we can renew our fast-dwindling supplies, we can start out all fresh and new on the last part of our journey. We will have come thirteen hundred miles from Independence. We will have only one thousand more to go."

When they rounded the mighty mass of Mt. Putnam, they looked off across the far-reaching plains of the Snake and saw the walls of the Old Fort. Then a shout would go up and even the very oxen that pulled the heavy wagons would seem to gain new strength and increase their speed.

Down the Ross Creek Valley they would go, and how short the ten or twelve miles would seem. How gratefully, as they splashed down into the waters of an intervening creek and up the banks on the farther side, would they come to rest in front of the old supply station, "The White Walled Fort."

The trading posts and the forts stood like mountain sentinels and havens of safety along the way. The men who traveled the plains were hardy and fearless. Yet they must often have longed for the rest, the safety of Old Fort Kearney there in Nebraska, Laramie, Bridger and Casper in Wyoming, and Fort Hall at the cross-roads of the trails in Idaho.

It was with something of that longing that, now traveling back over the Old Trail, we fixed our faces and sent our horses with springing step toward Fort Hall, still gleaming white in our imagination, on the banks of the Snake. It gave us a thrill to think that now, as we pursued our dream, we had passed out of Oregon and had come into Idaho.

Our first day's ride in Idaho was not long, something like twelve miles. We secured supplies at Parma and about five miles beyond came to a spot ideal for camping, a well-watered pasture and some little shrubbery around the fence from which we could gather a few handfuls of twigs for the fire. The owner of the ranch had just come through the gate and was closing it when we rode up and asked if it would be permissible to camp for the night. He surveyed us very carefully and somewhat critically. I guess the way had begun to tell on our equipment and our general appearance.

"What's your business"? he asked in rather a chilly and formal way.

We explained that we were riding the Old Oregon Trail and keeping as close to it as possible, and that this required grass for the horses.

"Riding the Old Oregon Trail, are you"? And, pulling the wire loop from the gate post, he threw the gate open, "Come in, come in, you are most welcome. We have heard about you. You are on the Old Oregon Trail right now. That little mound there marks the place where one of the first houses in these parts stood, a sort of supply place. The spring there is where they used to camp and water stock".

We spent Sunday camped in this pasture. Here the Old Trail had gone. Some fifty or sixty feet beyond was the new highway and, at about the same distance, the rails of gleaming steel over which the great Deisel engine would pull train after train through the livelong night. The Past was very near the Present. The Primitive was very near the Modern. which is better?

That night it was quite cold. Water was frozen in the collapsible bucket. A sack of oats was my pillow. If the conscience is clear and the body healthfully tired and the stomach comfortably filled, a sack of oats makes a pillow soft as down.

Before we rode away the next morning, Mr. Frank Frizzell of Caldwell, a special deputy sheriff, told us of a reception awaiting us at Caldwell. He also showed us one of the most strikingly ornamented Smith and Wesson revolvers I have ever seen. He was strangely cold however at my proposition to trade him my brand new 32 Special Winchester Carbine for it. Guess he could not carry the Carbine under his coat and under his arm.

At Caldwell we were graciously received, as we had been at every town we passed, and, after buying a curry-comb and supplies, we rode out to the Radio Station K C I D where we broadcasted a fifteen-minute interview. Then, putting on our slickers, we rode for six miles more through a steady rain and camped on the lawn at Wayne Naugle's Ranch. After a visit from two old War Buddies, Thomas H. Phelps and H. D. Hanks, whom I had not seen since the signing of the Armistice on November 11, 1918, and, after spending the evening going over the First World War again, but refusing to spend the night in the ranch house, we holed up in the snug little tent and the next morning rode into Boise.

Before we left the ranch, Mr. Naugle had mended the broken pannier, straightened out the badly-bent tent pegs, and put a sack full of oats on the Pack. He passed us on our way and went on into Boise, but that evening came to meet us just at the edge of town, in his arms our month's mail and a sack full of hot sandwiches. We stopped right there, read the mail, ate the sandwiches, and made camp for the night. We were happy and at peace with the whole wide world. We had received letters from home and checks large enough to provide supplies for our next month's travel. Some money in your pocket feels mighty good, though you may be going to ride in the desert.

Our campsite was near the junction of Route 20 and Route 30. Here Major Lugenbeil camped in 1863 on his way to establish the Boise Barracks. This had been a favorite camping ground of the early migration.

Here we were approached by a man who wanted us to advertise his tavern, by riding through the streets of Boise, with certain cardboard signs telling how long his business had been established, even before the Old Trail came through, he said. He really offered us very good wages. But at the devil's booth are all things sold, each ounce of dross costs its own ounce of gold. We did not need a meal ticket, as we still had plenty of bacon, eggs, and coffee; besides, our checks had come that day. We were finding, as the old pioneers had found, that we did not need much money on the trail but that we did need thick skins and a keen sense of humor.

Before we left, there came another man who wanted to trade horses. But here again no sale; we were in love with our own. Two other strange individuals came over to the camp the second evening; they were almost dwarfish in stature, and seemed to have a child's curiosity to know what these modern Indians looked like. Before the sun went down three children, on pinto ponies, visited us twice.

Thus the streams of life, which went by us as we camped down on these flats near the river, were varied and strange and in some ways positively ugly and forbidding, we were so interested in the historic things that we paid little attention to them except for now and then a little laugh.

We were very happy now, for after coming this far the horses seemed strong and in good spirits. It was real fun to watch Black Fairy run the full circle of her thirty-foot rope, then leap into the air, and come down stiff-legged, her head thrust down between her front feet. This she did time and time again.

That night and far into the night, we heard a radio from across the flat wailing out some very fuzzy music and we kept remarking,"Well, the old pioneer may have had to listen to the tom-toms and the war-whoops of the painted Indian, but they never had to listen to anything like this."

Somewhat sober and anxious, we resumed our journey the

next morning. We had been told that before us lay a stretch of seventy-five miles through a more or less desert country, mostly sagebrush, with few ranches along the way. We secured enough oats to ration the horses for three days and laid in a supply of bacon and eggs and flapjack flour for the same length of time. We figured on making about twenty-five miles a day. Well prepared, we pushed off, desert or no desert.

Our way led us up and around the bench on the west of Boise. What a view! What an attractive city this Boise. The cottonwoods were now out in all the exquisite color of their new tender leaves, and the morning was still fresh, bright, and sweet over the city. The grounds around the depot could not have been surpassed for artistic creation and color.

Just before reaching the depot, we were hailed by a fine, neighborly voice, that of the probate judge, Chalafant. He came out to greet us with the morning paper in his hands and to show us our pictures on the front page. The father of the judge was the first moderator of the Presbyterian Synod of the State of Idaho. We were coming at history in a very interesting way.

By the time the city was left behind and we had come out into the open country, we forgot all about the so-called desert. The scene before us was inspiring. The wide world just opened up before us. Here a marker placed in the actual rut of the Old Trail informed us that we were all O.K., on the right road, and just to keep on going, as the Old Timers just kept on going.

We remembered Whitman's words, "Travel, travel, travel, nothing else avails". This became our slogan and always started us going when we grew tired and when the way seemed long and the riding hard.

That night we camped out in the sagebrush a mile or more beyond a filling station, called Regina, near a deserted schoolhouse, half way between Boise and Mountain Home. We picketed our horses on scant grass and went to bed without washing our faces, and started traveling next morning without washing our faces, having used the water for evening and morning coffee. This we had to do several times on the summer's journey. Our camp was somewhat lonesome that night. We did not sit long about the campfire but turned in early. The deserted school looked sad and lonely and ghost-like in the dusk of the evening.

We had a hard time getting started the next morning. All three horses acted like they were demon-possessed. It was a battle to get the bridle on Dynamite. He had suddenly become aware that he had ears and was determined that they should not be touched. When the saddle was lifted to be thrown on his back, he would plunge aside, and when it finally found it's place, it was immediately bucked off. I thought for a time I had met my Waterloo, and that the big black had at last won the argument. Out of breath and downright tired, I paused a few minutes, rubbed the old fellow's head, then cautiously and slowly lifted the saddle in both hands and put it on his back. He had surrendered. He nervously twitched his hide as the saddle rested in it's place, but before he could change his mind, I had him cinched and ready.

The same scene was reenacted by Black Fairy , though it was not so long drawn out. Trouble, real trouble, started again with the Diamond. It was a job to get the blankets and the pack-saddle securely in place, but now I recalled a trick learned on a ranch in the early days. I simply tied a rope to one horn of the pack-saddle, lifted her right front leg and tied it up, then put on the panniers and started the diamond hitch before letting her leg loose. After resting briefly we mounted and started on.

All this day we rode in the rain, with the hoods of our slickers tied tightly under our chins. About four o'clock in the afternoon we passed through Mountain Home and camped at the J. E. Hunt ranch a few miles beyond. The wind was blowing hard and it was raining when we crawled into our sleeping bags.

When we started for Glenn's Ferry the next morning, Black Fairy tried to give her rider a bad few minutes. She kicked and jumped, and, had she been given her head, would have put on a bucking exposition. But Mrs. Beard was just too much for her and a few keen cuts with the riding crop on her hind quarters sent her on her way quite subdued. At five-thirty in the evening we rode into historic Glenn's Ferry.

Here we found there would be no place to picket the horses where they could have grass and water. So we gladly accepted the invitation of Wilbur Sellman to put them in his barn where they would be dry and warm. We did not put up the tent this night but spread our sleeping bags out on the sweet-smelling hay under an open-sided shed. It was a delightful place to rest. We could hear the horses eating, and once in awhile, they would call to us with sort of whispered neighs.

Glenn's Ferry is situated on the Snake River some two or three miles above the Two Island Crossing of the Old Trail. This, the first crossing of that turbulent stream, had presented a most difficult and dangerous obstacle. Moving from island to island, they found shallower parts of the river and the wagons were taken over. Several men lost their lives at this dangerous place, yet every following train drove down out of the hills, carefully weighed the chances, then fearlessly drove in and smashed through.

The same two long low islands are there today dividing the stream into three deep, swift, dangerous channels.

As we came down to the edge of the water, at the very place where the wagon trains came up out of the river, we felt very thankful that we did not have to cross as they had crossed. Here, somewhat later, a ferry was established by Mr. Glenn, and the town that grew up near by bears his name.

Mr. Glenn married an Indian woman and raised a family of four boys and two girls. Horace, Roy, Tom, Charlie and Myrtle and Leona. Horace was the oldest of the family. He is seventy-six years of age. He said that Old Timers would tell us where the Old Trail came across the river but that *he knew*. The Old Trail, in fact, did pass right by their home. Some Old Timers and Horace Glenn as well, showed us the trail, and, as they agreed, it must have gone where they indicated. We went down to the crossing, then followed it back across the flats for some miles, then up over a very steep and narrow ridge to the crest of the hills, where it struck out northwest and was lost in the sagebrush distance.

When the travelers came up out of the river and started for the hills across the flats, they were literally passing over acres of gold and knew it not. You can still see the old placer washings from which, it is said, hundreds of thousands of dollars in nuggets and dust were taken later. So, unknowingly, they had passed over the oil fields of Wyoming. So had they come the long reaches of the Platte and looked upon them as a desert to be crossed as quickly as possible. Since irrigation has come, long miles of it are a fertile garden of the Lord.

Here at this island ford or near it, Narcissa Whitman left behind the little trunk to which she had so lovingly and tenaciously clung across the wide and dreary plains. This treasured trunk was, in a very real sense, her hope chest. Her sister Harriet had given it to her as a parting gift. There must have been a real sorrow in her heart as she emptied it, then closed the lid, and bade it good-by, fondly patting it with her sunburned hands. But it is possible that the labor and danger of the Island Ford made it easier to part with one of the last treasures from the home she would never see again. When she saw the difficulty Marcus was having here at this place with his wagon; when she saw the wagon and the mules drawing it turned over and over in the swift flood, and knew that her husband had put his life in jeopardy in rescuing them and bringing them safely to land, her sacrifice of the trunk seemed a little thing.

It is very possible that when they came to the second and last crossing of the Snake at Fort Boise, not only the labors and dangers attending the crossing but the unselfish sacrifice of the trunk made it easier for Marcus to sacrifice his loved wagon and leave it behind. The wagon never reached the Mission. The little trunk never stood in her new little home in the west. As late as 1860 the wagon was known to be at the fort. Tom McKay salvaged the trunk for his own especial prize.

I have often wished Marcus could have taken the wagon through. I have often wished that Narcissa had locked her little trunk and then set it afloat as an Ark of Hope. Who knows? It might have gone through.

While at Glenn's Ferry we were also told that, at a place called Pilgrim's Gulch not far away, a terrible Indian massacre had occurred, and that even today we could find evidence of the battle, scraps of rusty iron, arrow heads, ox shoes and broken bits of glassware. We longed to visit the scene of this battle but time simply would not permit. However, near the ford, the lonesome graves of two men who were killed in this massacre can be seen today.

The old pioneers seemed not to have lingered at the island ford but hastened on across the flats up over the long, narrow ridge and were soon lost to sight behind the hills, as they set their faces, once again, toward the sunset.We would like to have lingered here for weeks, but we too had a long way yet to go. So we resolutely set our faces toward the sunrise.

It is a rough, rugged, lonesome country that one crosses going out of Glenn's Ferry toward Twin Falls and the White Fort beyond. On this way we first passed through a long stretch where, on both sides of the trail, the smooth and rounded boulders looked like bronze watermelons in some Iron Giant's garden. Then we passed along where a myriad of brown, gnarled, and twisted patches of rock, coming up out of the thin, scant soil, looked wrinkled and fevered like huge saddle sores on the scarred back of the earth. The three hundred miles lying between Fort Boise and Fort Hall, burning desert, sagebrush-covered and treeless, must have been a *Via Dolorosa* to women and children in the lurching, creaking conestoga wagons.

Passing through Bliss and dropping down below the rim rock, we came to a great spring pouring from the heart of the rock wall. Here the awful lonesomeness of the Snake River Country makes itself felt, and we began to realize the force and the power and the danger of the rapids of the Snake, which proved so terrible and almost fatal to the Wilson Price Hunt people of 1811-12. We had ridden twenty-nine miles that day, but came in singing and laughing. Here we found a cabin in a fenced-in pasture, a clear stream of cold, pure water cutting across one corner, with grass almost knee-high to the horses. We pitched our tent, made the fire, cooked our evening meal, and sat holding hands till darkness fluttered down and the silvery stars came out, looking into the west and into the supremely fascinating, but awful lonesomeness of the Snake.

The Hagerman Valley is one of the most fertile and interesting of all the country which lies along the Old Trail. We were prepared to enter into full enjoyment of it's unique fascination as we rode this day, for we got a happy start. Going out to catch the horses, we came upon the nest of a meadowlark not fifteen feet away from the tent. The mother bird, for some reason or other, had not been greatly disturbed at the proximity of her strange new neighbors. Then, too, we broke the only looking glass we had in our luggage and were quite disgusted at first, but when we started to shave, using the largest piece of the broken mirror, we were happily surprised to see that it reflected, in all it's full glory, the bright gladness of the rising sun.

All the broken mirrors of life, all the fractions of broken dreams and plans, will reflect the glory of the new rising sun if we will only turn them in the right direction. The nest of the meadowlark and the rising sun in the broken mirror sent us riding along into the sunrise with spring joy in our hearts and a song on our lips and with eyes fitted to see the goodness of the land through which we rode this day.

The Old Trail probably did not pass through Hagerman, though tradition says that it did, but it did pass not far away. We road through and camped in the Valley of the Thousand Springs, then on again through a vast irrigated garden and into the clean, proud, well-kept city of Buhl.

It is well that our start had been propitious, for our going through the morning was really tough. Once the pack horse got loose and started back over the trail toward Portland on a run. When we finally got her rounded up and turned back in the right direction, we found it was necessary to unload everything and readjust the pack. This we had to do twice more before the morning was over. Then, coming to an irrigation ditch, she plunged over it's steep sides, lay down and almost completely disappeared beneath the sluggish flowing water. This gave us a **real scare.**

We were tired, dirty, and hungry when we rode into Buhl, and were very happy when we found a restaurant and a great squared beam twenty or thirty feet in length, a hitching rail, a left-over from the days when all transportation was by wagon or saddle. To this we tied our horses while we had lunch.

We were fortunate to have the genial and kindly policeman

take the horses under his special care through the time we were eating. Here we met an Old Timer, Mr. Reeves, whose mind is just teeming with the stories and facts of the early days and the old trail. We talked with him for an hour. That evening he came over to the camp in the Fair Grounds at Filler and visited with us, where, with quite an audience of boys and girls, we went over the old days together.

Our camp at Filler was a perfect one with plenty of wood, plenty of water, lush tender grass, a most inviting place to pitch the tent under sheltering trees. The trees were full of birds singing us a most tuneful welcome and a happy good-night. At four o'clock in the morning we awakened from a dreamless sleep, with the delicious feeling that we were children again.

The ride to Twin Falls was uneventful, just pleasant going under warm and genial skies, through a highly cultivated garden, a remarkable change from the dust-covered, dreary country the pioneers passed through.

Always before us, away there to the northeast, the Saw Tooth Range called us on. At Twin Falls we had lunch with the Kiwanians and were made at home out at the grounds of the local riding club, through the courtesy of Mr. Cross of the Twin Falls Financial Corporation. There Black Fairy and the Dynamite were both shod on their front feet and there we witnessed some fine riding on the part of the members of the club.

Twin Falls will always be remembered as a home place by us two latter riders of the Old Trail. It is a very friendly city, it's people kind and generous. We shall never forget the hospitality of the E. G. Carroll family. The hearty good-by and good-luck shouted after us as we rode once more into the sunrise.

Soon after leaving Twin Falls, we turned aside to visit Shoshone Falls. The Wilson Price Hunt party in 1811 were probably the first group of white men ever to see these falls. And the grandeur and sublimity of the falls were lost to them because of the threat they and this turbulent stretch of the Snake offered to their progress to the sea. Every one of the thousands of emigrants who passed this way looked forward with great expectation to viewing their scenic wonder, even as we had looked for days. The falls in their rough and rugged canyon are awesome to even the satiated world travelers of today.

Looking down upon the steep and narrow canyon through which the river pours here at the falls, one can begin to realize what an awful barrier these canyons of the Snake must have presented to the Wilson Price Hunt people, who found such terrible and almost hopeless labor as they followed down their sides.

We crossed the Snake here on the high suspension bridge and traveled for miles through a well-irrigated country, with water flowing through the ditches everywhere. We camped by one of these irrigation canals that looked more like a baby river than the works of man. It seemed to meander here and there at it's own free will and to be singing to itself as it ran boiling over frequent rapids.

Here several people came over to the camp and spent the evening around the campfire. One of them, a woman whose grandparents had been among the first to come across the plains, told us a story of the early days. The pioneers had camped at Shoshone Falls for a rest and to do some washing. That night they became aware that something was wrong in the camp. There was some commotion among the livestock. Upon investigation it was found that the camp had been raided and the horses and mules stolen. So soon had the raid been discovered and the pursuit started that the thieves had not had time to take off the bell from one of the pack mules. By reason of the sound of the bell the pursuers were guided on the way and the thieves were rapidly overtaken. The old man called for the thieves to halt and, being disinclined to kill even a horse thief, he lifted his rifle and fired over their heads.

One of the thieves, frightened by the discharge of the gun, had fallen from his horse, but, landing on his feet and with nothing more than a bad fright, had disappeared into the sagebrush. The other, dropping the ropes by which he had been leading the stolen horses, put spurs to his own horse and faded away into the shadows of the night. In great glee the old man retured to camp with every one of his horses and mules. The laundry was in due time finished and, as though nothing more than a common thing had happened, the group hitched up and resumed their journey into the West. How interesting is life along the old trail.

Another story was of the construction of Milner Dam, a short way up the river from the falls. This account brought us back to the present day and modern life with its drama and heroic deeds. It was the story of a dream, a plan of action, then of seemingly insurmountable obstacles, then of grim inexorable determination, then of splendid success. The very bowels of the earth had been blasted into shreds, mighty machines had plowed out channels through the rocks as a plow furrows in mellow soil, and the life-giving water had been sent through those channels to spread out over the waste places.

The dam was just four miles from our camp. There and back would give us a nice leisurely ride of only eight miles. I was very anxious to ride out and see it, but Mrs. Beard wanted to do some washing (I just can't understand this obsession of women) and she had found the ideal place here at this irrigation canal, so she decided to stay by the stuff. I rode out alone. Solitude or aloneness has it's compensations, which in this case was a better acquaintance with the Dynamite. Never before had I learned the true greatness of this big black horse. With no pack animal to be pulled and worried along, he simply ate up the distance to the dam and back, and without wetting a hair on his glossy coat. And he liked it; he was truly like a free horse on his native range. The trail was good and free from loose stones; I gave him his reins. His head did not go down between his legs now but shot straight out, and, with a mighty leap, we were away with the speed of an antelope. He liked it and I liked it. There is no thrill that equals a ride on a good horse running free before the wind.

As I reached the dam and rode out half way before turning and looking up the river over the placid lake that now holds the awful gorge and terrible rapids of Caldron Linn within it's peaceful breast, and as I saw the water running so quietly through the great canal to flow out over the hundreds of thousands of acres of land, changing them into vast gardens, growing food for men, I observed to myself much can be said for the old followers of the trail, who explored and found their way across this vast land, but much, very much can be said for the New Pioneers, the engineers and the stout-hearted laborers who have spanned our plains with ribbons of steel, tunneled our mountains and chained our rivers.

Idaho has had her share of these giant-hearted men and much of Idaho today is as fair as the Garden of Eden itself.

To be honest, in this our story of the ride over the Old Oregon Trail, when I gave Old Dynamite his head and we raced toward the river, it was not so much the urge to see the engineering marvel of Milner Dam that drove us on as it was to see historic Caldron Linn.

This Caldron Linn in a very real way is a name that stands for the highest heroism, a name that tells of superhuman purpose and dauntless courage. This name takes us back one hundred and thirty-eight years. In 1811 the Wilson Price Hunt overland Astorians had left St. Louis early in the spring, by July reached far up the Missouri River into what is now the State of Montana, then turned south and west across two mountain ranges to Henry Fort on the headwaters of the Snake. They found the fort abandoned. They turned down the Henry Fork of the Snake. They lined their canoes down past Idaho Falls and through the rapids and down around American Falls. They were a merry bunch of out-door river men. Singing and laughing, shouting and calling to one another, as only real canoemen know how to do, they drove on. Old abandoned Fort Henry was now some three hundred and fifty miles behind them. Wild fowl of many varieties winged their way along the banks of the river, wild ducks, unaccustomed to the ways of man, oared into the little recesses and bayous of the stream to let the strange phantoms go unheeded by. The willows, cottonwood and wild flowers along the banks turned the stream into enchanting loveliness. A faint and faraway murmur fell upon their ears but it was utterly unheeded, or if heeded at all, it was only welcomed, for most of them were river men and a fast rapids was a thing to be welcomed rather than shunned; and every one, successfully passed, would bring them just a little nearer to their journey's end, the mouth of the Columbia, down at the sea and Astoria. No more weary traveling over rock ways on foot. No more weary packing and unpacking the horses.

The current of the river, almost unperceived, gathered headway as its banks narrowed and, suddenly, they were in the grip of the rapids. There was no blanching of their faces, scarcely a halt in their singing, old man river could do his worst. He would see who was master. They applied their paddles for increased speed and steering power and shot along with the speed of a diesel pulled train. One canoe plunged into the whirling, twisting, lashing rapids, another, the second one manned by Crooks, followed, was dashed upon a hidden rock, smashed, turned over, loosing all its load, and jettisoned its crew of five men into the savage turmoil. Five men were in the canoe when it hit. Four men reached shore. One man, the best canoeman of them all, the happiest voyager, the favorite of the band, was rolling along under the savage, snarling, wolfing waters.

Like frightened sparrows, the rest of the canoes darted to the shore.

Camp was made. There was no singing that night, nor for many a night, their minds and hearts were with that comrade whose body was being washed along on its lone, lonesome way toward the sea. When the surprise and hurt of the accident began to wear away, a council was held. Men were sent to explore the immediate reaches of the turbulent stream. Their report was against further attempts at reaching Astoria by canoe. Their decision was made. They would not return. They would go ahead. They had set their hearts toward the Sunset and they would drive their bodies to follow. They knew hardships, they had met death face to face, they had seen its ultimate power, they were not afraid. They might meet all these things again and again but there was Astoria by the sea, and there they would go. And go they did, and won through. They called this place Caldron Linn. This was on October 28, 1811. On February 15, 1812, in a burst of sunshine, they reached Astoria. They had conquered a continent. Caldron Linn — that means courage, dauntless, utter courage.

That night, after coming back from Caldron Linn, I could not sleep. A century and thirty-eight years were speaking to me. That dead man, Antoine Clappine, drowned at Caldron Linn, that group of half-dead, skeleton men, making their way down both sides of the Snake, kept calling back to me, "Little do we know what shall meet us across the plains of life, over the ranges, down through the gorges; little do we know, little does it matter, all that matters is to walk on, climb on, THERE IS ASTORIA BY THE SEA."

We planned to spend a quiet and restful Sunday in our snug wayfarer's home by the side of the canal at Greenwood, but about ten o'clock, two young people, Jack and Patsy Griffiths, both greatly interested in early history and especially in the Old Oregon Trail, came by and asked us to go with them to a dedication of some old building on the Trail just out of Hansen. As they had brought an official invitation for us to attend and have a part in the program, we, of course, consented.

Westward the course of empire takes its way, and it has used many methods of getting there. It has used several as it has traveled across the continent of America. It has gone on the feet of the natural explorer, who would be off and away, though he lived on the continent or in the valleys of the moon. It has gone with the fur-trader, the Indian scout, the pioneer in his ox-drawn wagon, the pony express, the stage coach, the express trains, the mighty ships of the air. All of these ways met this day at Hansen.

The ranch home and the building that was dedicated for historic purposes had seen three of them used. It was a trading post and supply station at first, the first trading post erected west of Fort Hall. Many an Indian, many a trapper and trader, many a traveler over the Old Oregon Trail, that ran about fifty feet from its door, had stopped here and secured the things needed. A horse thief had been shot on the trail near here and had fallen as he had started into the house to have some one of the kindly inmates bind up his wounds; his blood had run over one of the big, flat rocks that made the walk up to the kitchen door. At another time, the store itself had been robbed by bandits. The pony express building was made of heavy hewn logs and was still livable. Ben Holliday used this pony express building for one of the stations on his stage line.

But let the marker that was unveiled that day tell the story. It says,

Rock Creek Station

Original Building was Erected by James Bascom in 1865. It was sold to Herman Stricker in 1876. The First Trading Post West of Fort Hall. Station for Pony Express and Ben Holliday Stage Line. The Largest Artery of Wagon Travel in United States Passed Here on the Old Oregon Trail in 1884. This Building was Donated by Mrs. Lucy W. Stricker on Her 83rd Birthday.

Twin Falls County Company.

From our pleasant camp on the Greenwood Canal, the trail led out into a land that had abruptly changed from a fertile, irrigated garden into a vast, lonely desert, with nothing but the sullen sagebrush on every hand, and with only a few frightened jackrabbits to relieve the monotony of slowly passing hours. However, before the day was done, we came back again to the water-filled canals and fertile fields and camped at night on the west bank of the Snake, just beyond Rupert.

As usual, when we were near a town or a highway, we had many visitors. At Rupert the mayor, Mr. Brazil, and a delegation from the Chamber of Commerce gave us a hearty welcome, assisted us in securing much needed supplies for ourselves and horses, and came out in the evening with Mr. Howard Moffett and wife to make us a visit. As we sat around the fire spinning yarns, two real cowgirls raced up on their ponies, set them back on their haunches, in true western style, dismounted, and joined our happy group at the fire, and what a splendid picture they made — Doris Klickert, tall and blonde lassie, and Olive Acock, a comely little brunette, sitting with cowboy hats shoved back from their foreheads and hands outstretched to the genial warmth of the fire, and teeth gleaming white in the glow of the leaping flames.

We were very glad when sunset brought the end of this day's ride, for though we had come back into an irrigated district and had ridden for several miles over a magic carpet tacked down with a myriad of wild flowers, and gladdened by so many fresh golden dandelions that we called it the ride down the dandelion trail, our horses had been restless and hard to handle. This was noticeably true of the Black Fairy, who insisted on being frightened at every tumbleweed that moved in the wind, and at every sheep or calf that moved across a pasture, or any bird that would fly up out of a cluster of weeds. She seemed to have an insane desire to run away.

Our troubles did not end when we went into camp, however. The animals had scarcely been staked out when something, perhaps a rattlesnake, frightened Black Fairy. She began to plunge like mad, and broke loose from the rope and started to run away. Black Diamond, joining in the excitement, plunged wildly and, coming up shortly at the end of her rope, turned a complete summersault and lay for a time squarely on her back, with all four feet wildly pawing the air. Certainly she looked ludicrous, and we laughed in spite of it all. Just then, Dynamite also joined in the confusion and broke loose and started out on a run. But for the aid of two men, who, providentially happened along in the nick of time, and helped round up the two horses, we would have been afoot out there on the old trail. However, we rounded them up, tied them on shorter ropes, gave them an extra two quarts of oats apiece, to compensate them for the grass they would lose on their short tether, and were in pretty calm and peaceful mood by the time our first visitors arrived.

As I lay awake for some time that night, an old Latin phrase kept coming to my mind, *"Forsan et haec olim meminisse iuvabit,"* which I translated, "perhaps to remember these things will give pleasure sometime." It has. I have also noted that the things, which seem to be remembered with greatest satisfaction and joy by the old pioneer, when his mind goes back to faroff ways to days that are no more, are not the easy stretches of the trail, the pleasant miles driven, but of the hard things, labors, difficulties, and narrow escapes from death itself.

We were to have many of these hard things which would bring us that future joy. Two of them came as we resumed our journey, with Raft River as our day's objective. Our way again led through a desert. Some years ago, a far-reaching fire burnt off even the sparsely growing sagebrush, leaving the ground barren and white. Toward the south, it suddenly seemed that some giant had flung out a heavy gray blanket and was waving it up and down and back and forth. Almost as soon as we were aware of the approaching storm, it was upon us. Thin wisps of sand, like heavy lint whipped from the cracking folds of the blanket, swept with stinging fury across the trail, and then the blanket itself entirely enveloped us. The sun disappeared in the pall of swirling sand, and then night; neither dark nor light; drab, somber, ghostlike, was at hand. The horses stopped, turned their backs to the storm, dropped their heads between their front legs and refused to move. They soon looked like gray rocks standing in a weltering sea of murky spray. The trail faded into a faint threadlike line which we could barely recognize through the thin slits of our squinting eyes. We could scarcely see and were even finding it hard to breathe in this pitiless smother. We took our handkerchiefs, wet them thoroughly with the water from our canteens, and held them over our faces and breathed through these improvised filters till the worst of the storm had passed.

When the first fury had spent itself, we wiped the sand from our eyes and ears, cleansed our throats with the remaining water from our canteens and started, crawling along, like desert rats, for the waters of the Raft River.

Well, it was good, when, after some two hours of miserable riding, we came completely out of this desert nightmare into the calm and clear sunshine of what promised to be an evening of peace and quiet. Out on the crest of the plateau we looked down on a long-stretching hill and across the wide green valley of the Raft. That green valley was surely an alluring place for camping and we camped early.

As soon as the horses were tethered, they began to roll over and over and over again as if trying to get the sand out of their coats. The mistress hastily began preparing the evening meal and I began cleansing the duffel. I took a towel and wiped the saddles till every flower on the rich, red, hand-tooled leather blossomed again. I cleansed the bridle bits and even wiped the cinches and ropes of the pack saddle. I was doing a fine and a very happy job of it and with much satisfaction to myself, but when I took up the saddle blanket and gave it a shake, sending out a cloud of dust, and the mistress called out, "Cut it out, we've had enough desert dust today, without having it for dinner." I obeyed with cheerful alacrity, calling it a day.

Troubles never come singly or alone, they say, and we guess the saying is so. We, at least, found it so that night. Our troubles were not yet over, for threatening clouds covered the setting sun, and faraway rumbling and thunder came faintly across the hills. Just as we crawled into our sleeping bags, a mighty electric storm swept the valley. It seemed as if the crashing thunder would shake down the tent and that every flash of the jagged and forked lightning would shrivel it into ashes.

We were now, in very fact, experiencing one of the truly awe-inspiring events that so often brought terror to the women and children who crossed the plains in their canvass covered wagons. They would leave Independence, there on the banks of the Missouri, as early in the spring as possible, by the first of April at least. The grass would be turning green at this time. It was necessary that they follow the spring into the West, for the grass was the raw stuff of their motive power, the absolutely necessary food for mule, horse, or oxen. But the spring also brought the awful storms of rain and hail and winds of cyclonic power. Often these cyclones or tornadoes would sweep down upon them with terrible and sudden swiftness. Sometimes, the wagon, anchored to the ground by great chains with stakes driven deep, would withstand the fury, at other times the stakes would snap like splinters or be pulled loose and the wagons overturned and smashed into wrecked heaps upon the prairies. Many times the canvas roof stretched over the bent hickory bows would be simply lashed into shreds by the force and fury of the winds. Often, in these storms, the cattle would stampede and could be rounded up and the journey resumed, only after many precious days travel had been lost. These storms, which they encountered on the prairies, were truly terrible ordeals.

They were endured, however, as but one of the many disagreeable things that come in life. After every storm they simply hitched up and drove on with a song. The thunder, the lightning, the wind were awe-inspiring to us.

It took all our rock-ribbed, Presbyterian faith to lie in the frail tent which sheltered us and calmly assure ourselves that the disturbance would soon pass, and whatever happened it would be all O.K. We did draw some comfort from the knowledge that we need not fear the crash of thunder, we had just heard, for the great projectile had then been fired and could do no harm, and if lightning did strike, we would not know it anyway. Yet I found myself making a resolve that I would never undertake another journey like this till I could find a thunder-proof tent, and one impervious to the flash of lightning.

Here at Raft River the trails of the early day met and parted. Ashley and his men reached this river and trapped here as early as 1824 or 1827. Jennie Broughton Brown in her book on Fort Hall tells us that a band of free trappers, under a man named Russell, reached here in 1838. Fremont, in his second journey of exploration, reached this river some time in 1843 and traveled some distance along the Raft River road toward California, then turned and came back to the Snake and resumed his trek toward the Columbia.

While lying awake and listening rather uncomfortably to the fury of the maelstrom that was seething through the air outside the tent, I began to recall these historic facts. As the pioneer had often done, I began to weigh the possibilities of the trails that met them here. When they came out from Fort Hall, they found two trails, one leading to California, the other leading north and west to the Willamette Valley, which was the objective of most of the emigrants as they left Independence. Now they were seriously divided in mind whether to keep on going or to turn south into California. They spent many sleepless hours making the final decision.

Before us, also, three ways opened. One south to California and to a ranch home far away in the hills of southern California and three little grandsons who would welcome us there. One lay back along that same Old Oregon Trail which

Fremont had taken and there awaiting us our comfortable home and a host of friends. The other lay straight east into the sunrise with our next objective the White Fort on the Snake, under the frowning brow of Mt. Putnam.

Our foolish old sentimental hearts were urging the California Trail and the gold of love that lay there in the hills. Our really tired bodies were crying out loud, take the way back home over the Old Oregon Trail, leading into the deep, cool forests and the clear sparkling rivers that flow down from the heights of Hood. But our dream of some fifty years or more with it's glorious expectation was calling, ride on into the Sunrise and the White Fort is not very far away. We rode on into the Sunrise and toward the White Fort. It may have been an inferiority complex on our part that made the decision. I am no psychologist and do not intend to explore the reason for it, but this I do know; half asleep, half awake, I seemed to see that little shrivelled-up shrimp of a cow-poke that had made me so mad away over in Oregon at the beginning of our journey. He came riding by jauntily, a sarcastic smile was on his face, he seemed to rein in his horse and stop. Then, he said, "So, you are getting pretty tired, arent you? Want to turn back, and give it up, don't you? You are not ready to pay the price of real hardship to get through. Why don't you turn back? It is a long way to Independence. In fact, you are just getting started. It is a long way. I know I can ride it, but I don't think you can".

I immediately answered, "You little shrimp, you little weazoned son of nothing, I'll bet you this big, two-bladed jack-knife, I can ride the very pants off you. Come on, let's go".

I honestly and frankly think and say, I doubt very much whether we would ever have endured the tiredness, the hardships, and gotten through had it not been for the gratuitous insult the strange cowboy had offered to me over there near Echo at the beginning of the ride. Next morning, by eight o'clock, we were all saddled up, and moved out on our way toward Old Fort Hall.

American Falls was the next town along the trail that we were anxious to see. Again, the trail led up a long, long hill and straight ahead into a somewhat desert country, then into a wheat belt, dry farmed, then into a section more rugged and picturesque, with here and there a dwarf juniper growing, and finally we came out where we could look down upon the Snake, fascinating, alluring, inevitable as fate, lonesome.

Near noon, we arrived at Rock Creek Emigration Camp near Massacre Rocks. This historic spot has been turned into an inviting park. Leaving the horses tethered to a post at the gate, we went over to the pump at the concrete-sealed well; washed our faces, hands, arms and breasts with the pure cold water; sat down and rested for a time; then ate our lunch.

We were anxious to get to this place, for we had been here twenty-five years before and had found the head of an Indian and the head of a white man, which resembled the picture of Buffalo Bill, etched on one of the big boulders, and wanted to see if they were still here and if we could find them. We were not disappointed, there they were as plain, as legible as they were a quarter of a century ago, and as we suspect they will be for many of a quarter century to come.

When we located the rock for which we were looking, we came back to the great boulder on which hundreds of names have been etched. The oldest inscription we could find was one of 1849. Many of the names have grown so dim, the dates so faint, they cannot be read. The wild roses were growing around the base of Register Rock in the crevices of it's sides. Perhaps they will be growing here when the last name disappears from the rock. Why should the spirit of mortal be proud; when we are here today and gone tomorrow, and our very names, cut into the hardest of granite, last for only a few, brief years at the best? Soon, over all, the briars and brambles and the wild roses will grow.

Going back to the gate where the horses were tethered, we sat down to rest for awhile. As we sat there the past, or, at least, a day of the past, came before us as a dream. It was August 10, 1862, a wagon train of that never ending flood of West-faring men came slowly moving through a narrow gorge in the bronz hills there in the east. Suddenly came the wild, blood-curdling cry of Indians on the path of war; there was the twanging of many a taught bow released, the shrill crack of answering rifles, the screams of frail women, the cry of frightened children, the rumble of wagon wheels speeded up by the stampeding oxen, and the massacre, which gave it's name to this picturesque spot, was over. The wild Shoshone had killed nine white men of the train and wounded six.

At the east side of the valley, we passed through the narrow pass where the Indians had ambushed this wagon train. It was an ideal spot for the fiendish deed. So Massacre Rocks it is today. Pondering the uncertainty and the brevity of mortal life, we rode the rest of our thirty mile stint for the day and camped with some real Indians near the bridge over the Snake at American Falls.

The horses seemed real fresh and both Mrs. Beard and myself felt pretty cheerful. We seemed to have gotten our sea legs, or saddle knees, and were not too tired after the two fairly long rides of thirty miles on two successive days.

When we went over to the water hydrant, near which the Indians were camped, one of the young squaws rather cheerfully told us, "He broke." So we carried water from the filling station a couple of blocks away.

All evening long, a meadowlark sat on a post just beyond our camp singing it's cheery song. We had not had a single day, since leaving home on the first day of April, without a song.

This was the twentieth day of May. We were delayed in our start by a visit from two charming, young women, one a reporter for the *Desert News*.

When we stopped at the service station to give the horses their morning drink, we found that the pack had suffered a bad rope burn on her left hind foot. We washed it out with clean, cold water and moved on. That night we washed it again, then swabbed it with warm bacon grease. It began to heal and caused us little trouble.

As we came into Pocatello , we were met by some newspaper men, who, after interviewing us, and taking some pictures, informed us that arrangements had been made for us to camp at the fair grounds and that oats for the horses could be secured at the Tillman Riding Academy.

We had just arrived at this destination when we witnessed what might easily have been a tragedy. One of the horses had thrown his rider, had leaped over a high fence and was almost run down by a speeding auto. The horse was roped and brought back. The only casualty was a pretty badly scarred-up Westen saddle.

That night we were visited by a great many friendly people, by several newspaper men and a photographer. The pictures taken of the tent and campfire were not so bad. We could hardly sleep that night, for tomorrow we would go out to the place where Old Fort Hall, "The White Fort," of the emigrant's dream and of our own dream, had stood.

As the old emigrant used to stop at Fort Hall for rest and refreshment and to replenish his dwindling supplies, so we made Pocatello our supply fort.

Our first errand was to the post office where we secured mail from home with checks for our monthly expenditures. Then we went to the store for some new Levis (we both needed them) the others had grown dangerously thin. My hat had grown just too tough looking for even a rider of the trail to keep on his head. So we bought another, a nice, nifty-looking Stetson, and a final purchase, some stockings for Mrs. Beard, some soap, some medicine for the horses and some films for the camera. Then to the hotel for a good steak dinner. This really was about parallel to the Whitmans, who regaled themselves with new-made bread at Old Fort Hall. Up to this time we had eaten so much bacon that, at every meal, we had promised ourselves a change when we got to town.

After dinner we contacted Dr. Minnie Howard and Mr. W. P. Havenor, county surveyor, two persons deeply interested in historical things, especially of the Old Oregon Trail and of Fort Hall. They arranged to take us out to Fort Hall the next day.

By the time I had taken the horses to the blacksmith to have them shod all around, our friends had arrived, we were picked up and with a reporter from a Salt Lake newspaper, were taken out to the long-desired place.

It is now a lonesome spot, some eight or ten miles off the highway, down on the flat near the river—somewhat nearer the river than in the old days, for the Snake has changed it's bed, perhaps several times, since the building of the fort by N. J. Wyeth in 1834. Wild grass grows now, tall and luxuriant, where the buildings once stood, and where the white-winged wagons were parked. There is a marker erected here by Ezra Meeker, who was very sure of the location.

As we stood looking at the rise in the ground that plainly showed a rectangular outline where the outer walls stood, and at the depression on the northeast corner — probably rifle - pits for the outer defense — the historians, Dr. Howard, Mrs. Hall and Mr. Havenor, began to recall many of the stirring events that had happened here and to name over many of the historical characters that had visited the Old White Fort.

On August 5, 1834, something like an American flag was raised above it's walls. Wyeth sold it to the Hudson's Bay Company in 1836 and, in 1837, they took possession. Francis Ermatinger was the first Britisher in charge from 1838-42, then Richard Grant.

It had been established as a supply station, the third one built on the Old Trail and one of the most important. Fort Laramie and Fort Bridger were the other two. Here Jason Lee had come with Wyeth and on Sunday morning, July 26, 1834 preached the first sermon ever preached in the Pacific Northwest. Next day he officiated at the funeral services of Kanseau, a Frenchman, who had been thrown from his mount in a horse race and instantly killed.

Here Kit Carson had come, Narcissa Whitman had come, longing for the bread her mother used to make. And she found a well-balanced dinner of buffalo meat, vegetables from the garden, and bread; the bread probably in the form of scones or bannock, baked on the griddle or in a skillet. Here she had rested on the rough benches and recruited her strength for the further exacting labors of the journey. Here Miles Goodyear deserted Marcus Whitman, to avoid the continued service which all the laws of gratitude would seem to have required.

When Whitman was preparing to leave Fort Hall after a short rest, eager to be on his way to Fort Boise, some three hundred miles along the final stage of the journey to Walla Walla, Goodyear delivered the ultimatum that Whitman would either have to abandon the last of his two wagons (one was already resting beside the trail back at Fort William) or else abandon him. Whitman decided in favor of the cart. For this Whitman was truly admirable.Why should this stripling, this waif dictate to a man like Whitman? Miles Goodyear owed faithful service to Whitman, the great, though hard-boiled missionary, to the very end of the way. Whitman had found him at the start of his journey back near Leavenworth, half naked, half starved, sick, armed with an empty rifle, no powder in the horn, no bullets in his pouch, worn-out shoes on his feet, but with heart set toward the West; gave him food, clothing, protection, brought him this far on the way. Wagon or no wagon, Miles Goodyear's place was by Marcus Whitman's side.

Well, he chose what seemed the less difficult way. He prospered in a certain manner. He was the first to grow produce in the Salt Lake Valley. He built up a great ranch where Ogden now is. The Donner party passed within thirty miles of his ranch, but missed it and so missed the supplies that might have meant the saving of their lives. He married an Indian girl and raised his family, staked a gold claim of fabulous value on the Yuba River in California, became a well-known Mountain Man and finished his career in the very noontime of life. He was only thirty-two years of age when he died. Somehow, we wish he might have stayed with Whitman.

Here, then, stood this old supply station, this old fort at the crossways of primitive Indian trails and at what was later to be the cross-trails and road of half a continent. With it's adobe walls, white-washed and gleaming, it had stood as a Mecca to travelers of the early day. Here it stood, and here it witnessed the drama of drunken debauchery and pure, spiritual religion, of eternal loyalties and disgraceful desertions. Here it stood, witness to the eternally fascinating drama of life.

Standing at this historic spot, which, for long years had been the Mecca of our own dreams, and listening to these stories coming up out of the past, we began to long for some little token, some artifact, that would prove conclusively to ourselves that the Old Fort stood here.

"I wish I might have a spade or something with which to dig in this storied plot of ground", I said to Mr. Havenor.

"Well. Chaplain, if you are looking for work, I can accommodate you," said he, and going to his car, he brought out a spade, and, putting it into my hands, said, "Well, get busy".

Feverishly beginning to dig, I made a hole about three feet wide and two or two and a half deep, unearthing some wood that had evidently been part of one of the logs of the old building.

It is said that the original structure, the American Old Fort Hall, was in form some sixty feet square and that it was constructed of cottonwood logs. These logs were twelve feet in length and set two feet deep in the ground. Quarters for the men and the goods were built inside the larger walls. Provisions were made for defence by constructing two bastions where armed men could command the approaches to the fort. It was evidently some part of this old, original structure from which the rotten wood had come.

A few shovels more and a thrill like an electric shock passed over me, for the blade of the spade had struck something of a metallic nature. From the dirt and gravel, where it had been buried for perhaps nigh on to a hundred years, we pulled out a great, square-linked log chain, six or eight feet long, if it could have been untangled from it's rust-congealed folds. After that we found a part of a great hinge, then some bands of iron, that had once been around the hubs of a Conestoga wagon. We were all very sure now that the Old White Fort had stood there.

Dr. Howard and Mr. Havenor both gladly suggested that these artifacts should be sent to the University to be kept among other relics of that time when the Old Fort had stood at the cross-trails of half the continent.

Next day, we passed through the Indian Agency, turned the heads of our horses up Ross Creek, took the Old Trail around the mighty bastion of Mt. Putnam. Here the old trail would lead us down into the Portneuf Valley, through the Falkner ranch, through Chesterfield and over some forty miles to Soda Springs.

VII

CAMP OF THE RAINBOW

WE HAD BEEN EAGER TO REACH THE White Fort; we were just as eager to be on our way again. The words of Whitman kept coming to our minds, "Travel, travel, travel; this alone matters; this alone will get you over the way." They could make twelve to fifteen miles a day, when we could make twenty to thirty, yet time was relentlessly pressing us as it did them. Two thousand miles, or rather two thousand five hundred miles (for we were going down by the way of Fort Bridger at the extreme southwest corner of Wyoming and would take several side trips back and forth across the trail) — is a long ride on horseback.

On Monday morning, we made an early start from Pocatello. Following the old freight road along the hills east of the highway, we reached the town of Fort Hall at noon. We ate lunch here with a fine old Indian, Frank Randall, whose clear, powerful mind could readily call up stirring images out of the past. His real sense of humor made his stories most fascinating. He had lived near Fort Hall long before Pocatello was founded. I wanted to pay for the dinner but he insisted on going Dutch. I felt better when a little Indian lad, who held our horses while we ate, smilingly accepted the silver dollar pressed into his chubby brown fist.

After lunch we traveled back to Ross Creek, then turned east and all afternoon followed the actual Old Trail north of Mt. Putnam. At the summit of the pass we found a delightful alder grove, with a clear mountain stream singing along through grass-covered flats, ideal for our camp.

A red winged blackbird circled the tent. A robin flew up and perched on a wild rose vine. The wind came now in small gusts and dispersed the smoke of the campfire in lacy blue films. The smell of the bacon frying in the pan and the odor of rich, brown coffee boiling in the pot, added their share to the sense of well-being which stole through our hearts.

I had come into camp angry and tired. Within two miles of camp, the Pack had laid down, rolled on the panniers, and dislodged them both. The whole load had to be taken off, re-adjusted and securely tied with the "diamond hitch" within half an hour of the close of the day. Now, Mrs. Beard called, "Come and get it;" the dainty lunch was spread in perfect order on the red-checked tablecloth; the blackbird's note and the robin's song had stolen into my heart. I felt so sorry for getting angry with the Pack that I went out and put my arms around her neck and asked her to forgive me for being angry. She put her tired head over my shoulder and stood still, slightly caressing my cheek with her soft, damp muzzle. I think any conscience could have slept well that night.

Arising about two o'clock, I went out of the tent to make my usual inspection. Things were utterly still. Not a leaf was quivering on the trees. A benignant moon stood above the mountain; the horses, standing motionless, were looking up at its radiant splendor.

Next morning we had to pass through a great flock of sheep which were already on the way to new feeding grounds. The herder rode a spirited sorrel horse, much finer than a sheep herder generally rides. We found that it belonged to the young lad who was driving the wagon at the rear of the flock.

Owing to the wrong directions or to misunderstanding of the right directions, which were given us by another sheep herder to whose wagon we had gone for information, we got entirely off the Old Trail and rode some five or six miles out of the way. When we had retraced our steps into the Portneuf Valley, we camped about a hundred yards west of the river.

Here we found high, well-drained ground on which to set up the tent. We carried water over one of the softest and brightest carpets the feet of man ever touched. The Portneuf Valley at this place is truly enchanting.

At noon the next day we reached the Faulkner Ranch. At this spot a marker shows where the Old Trail crossed the river, ran through the ranch, and began to climb to the west and around the north of Mt. Putnam. Here I lost my cherished jack-knife. I replaced it with a somewhat poorer substitute when I arrived at Soda Springs.

We followed the trail southeast through Chesterfield. Here, on Old Dynamite, I rounded up two horses which had broken out of a pasture and were threatening to disappear over the hills. The young lady, their owner, seemed very grateful when we drove them back. Old Dynamite stepped proudly, seeming to know that he had done his good deed for the day.

Black Diamond pulled her usual stunt this day by lying down in the creek and rolling over with the pack. It was truly a laughing sight to see the water dripping down from her head and running in streams from the panniers. I think she was startled and a bit frightened at the depth of the water. We were in good humor about it all, for her load held and did not have to be readjusted. We felt that we were getting expert with the "diamond hitch."

About six miles south of Chesterfield we camped by a creek. We would have loved to remain in this ideal camping spot, but Soda Springs was not far away, and there we went. We were directed to the historic camping spot. Here is a park and a fine log cabin, just the sort of accommodation a rider of the trail would desire. We did not pitch our tent but slept in the cabin. There was a stove with it's pipe stuck out through the wall. We felt quite modern cooking supper on it. After the meal was over, we swept out with a broom made of sagebrush. It left a good many powdered gray leaves, but it filled the room with a delicious, pungent odor. With the house work finished, we went down to the big soda spring. It is said that the trappers, Mountain Men and early emigrants used to get drunk on its water. We do not believe it, for after drinking quarts of it, we could still write our diary and had no throbbing heads the next morning.

Soda Springs would make an ideal situation for a permanent circus. One need only supply lemons and sugar and have all the lemonade he could drink for less than a nickel. Wish I could have found this spot when I was a boy.

Coming out from the town to the spring, we passed through a severe electric storm. The flashes of lightning seemed to strike at the very feet of the horses. Black Fairy, terribly frightned, reared and tried to escape from each flash. Mrs. Beard had to do some pretty skillful riding to control her.

OLD TRAIL MARKER, NEAR BURNS, OREGON

A DOG JOINS OUR PARTY FOR A WHILE AT LIME, OREGON

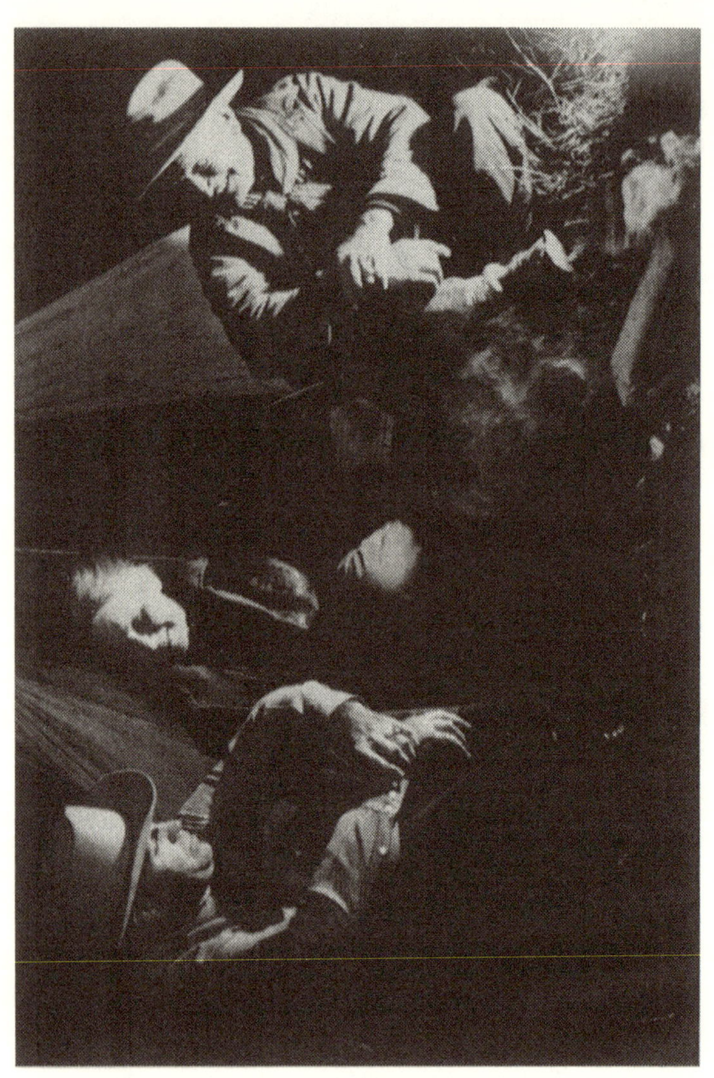

CAMPFIRE, NEAR OLD FORT HALL

The lightning struck just a short way to the north, and killed a young lad who had left his tractor and was crossing the fields to his house.

Leaving Soda Springs the next morning, we passed through a new-washed land, and the rain continued. When we rode into Georgetown, where the Old Trail followed the main street, we had on our hooded slickers and looked like a couple of pretty tough clansmen. However, we did not terrify the mayor and the good old Mormon bishop, who gave us permission to camp in the ball park, a part of the acreage around the church and school. He stipulated only that we keep the horses off the church sidewalk and porch.

This day we caught our first sight of Bear River, famous in the days of the trapper, the fur trader, and the pioneer. Just before we came to Montpelier, Black Fairy put on a rather spectacular exhibit, rearing and plunging and finally falling heavily and rolling over. I was badly frightened and terribly concerned for Mrs. Beard, but she landed squarely on both feet. Mounting again, as unconcerned as if it all went in a day's work, she led the three-horse train into Montpelier. Here a car with a loud speaker welcomed us and invited us to a dance that night. No sale.

A kindly old-time resident of the town, Mrs. Josephine Driver, invited us to picket our horses on her front lawn while we ate dinner. A quick sale. A Mr. Lloyd instructed us how to find the Old Road over the hills and invited us to camp at his son's ranch on the other side. Another quick sale.

The six miles over the Emigrant Pass was serious going. It had not been traveled for years. The water washing down through the century had made it almost impassible. At one place we found the side of the ravine along the trail too steep for the horses, so we crossed the deep-washed gulley to the other side. Riding down through an aspen thicket, we became tangled in a mesh of rusty, barbed wire fencing. We escaped the wire with only minor cuts on the limbs of the Pack.

Then we headed back across the gully, to find a narrow ledge not more than two or three feet wide, with deep ditches on both sides. Down this I turned Old Dynamite, who walked it something like a tight-rope walker, watching each step very carefully. Here his life on the range made him native again. The Pack, now loose, followed just as carefully and Black Fairy came last. Looking back, I could see that Mrs. Beard's face was white, her lips were closely pressed together, and her jaws were grimly locked. She had a look of absolute determination.

At the Lloyd ranch, we were heartily received by it's owner, the good mistress, and the four little daughters. It was Saturday night and they urged us to spend the Sabbath day with them. We turned the horses loose in the pasture of one hundred and sixty acres, knowing they would come when called for oats. They celebrated their freedom with a wild race, Black Fairy in the lead, Old Dynamite second and the Pack last. Reaching the other side, they stopped and looked back, with heads and tails high in the air.

We spent Sunday climbing the high ridge over which the Old Trail had first left the valley. We found where the stones had been thrown aside to make the going easier. We saw the holes where treasure seekers later had been hunting for buried gold.

There is a tradition that a party of soldiers in charge of forty to seventy thousand dollars worth of gold (the story differs) had been attacked by a band of Indians where the trail came down over the west side of those hills and that only one man had escaped. The gold is supposed to have been buried just before the attack. We were told that the remains of some half-burned wagons could still be found there, but an all day search showed not a trace of gold, battlefield, or wagon.

We heard a romantic story of this young rancher who as a boy had herded sheep for a wealthy uncle, but becoming restless, had left the job. He covered quite a stretch of western territory, working on farms, in mines, in lumber camps. When the wanderlust had died out, he returned to the home ranch, expecting to continue his old job, but was informed that his services would no longer be needed, and that he had better strike out on his own.

This he did. Then he truly began to understand life. He went to work at the first thing that came to hand, until something better appeared and changed to it, all the time saving every red cent. He bought a ranch, going in debt for it, but stocking it with cattle bought with his earnings. When we were at his place, he was running some five hundred head of cattle. He had his fine, thrifty wife and four healthy children.

He was a Mormon boy and believed his religion. Let me hasten to say, I have never found a more kindly, generous, considerate people in all my travels, than I found among the Mormons, both in the 346th Machine Gun Battalion in the First World War, when I was their chaplain, and on this long journey through Idaho and Wyoming, where I was often their invited guest.

We left this home reluctantly, and started the four-mile ride that took us across the border into Wyoming. It was now the last day of May. We rode through the Emigrant Gap over a vast carpet of green and gold, patterned with dandelions. We found white, pink and crimson flowers here which looked like bouquets that bridesmaids sometimes carry. Someone told us that they were the Desert Primrose, the blossoms lasting only for a day, white in the morning, pink at noontime, red at night. We did not try to prove it; some things are more beautiful without the support of scientific facts.

We were rather dispirited when we came to Cokeville. We had planned to get supplies but found the town tightly closed. They were celebrating their three days of Memorial Service. But we have since greatly enjoyed a story we heard of how Sage and Cokeville had been scrambled in the early days. It was told us by Charles J. Deloney ,whom we met in the Sears Roebuck store in Portland. He had lived in this part of Wyoming and had heard the story as a boy.

It seems that at the place named Sage there were some coke ovens and at Cokeville there was quite a stretch of sagebrush. When the railroad was being put through, some one of the crew was given two signs to mark the two different places where depots were to be built, and the signs were to be put up descriptive of the places. But the man who had the matter in charge had become somewhat woozy from drinking "Mountain dew", and swapped the signs. Mr. Deloney did not vouch for the authenticity of the story, nor do I, but I do know that corn liquor can engineer some strange scrambles in life.

We also heard how something like a hundred thousand dollars was spent trying to bring in an oil well at Sage, with no returns. As we passed through, we found it one of the deserted ghost towns of the West. It's chief sign of life being a construction train, with it's box car living quarters for the crew pulled up on the side track.

Camping by an irrigation ditch, some four miles out, we had a rather amusing experience. Three men, very noticeably under the influence of this same "mountain dew", came by and wanted to trade horses. They looked our horses over, inspected their feet and opened their mouths to see their teeth—all without asking permission. One of them seeing the crosses on my collar, came up and said, "Father, I would like to shake hands with you." Then looking at Mrs. Beard, he added in rather staccatto syllables, "Could I—shake—hands—with—her?"

"Why, yes, I don't think she would object," I said.

After shaking hands with her, he came back to where I was standing and, putting his arm about my neck, reached over and whispered in my ear, "Father, I am a Catholic and these other two fellows are Mormons; you can't trust them, be careful what you say to them."

He had scarcely moved his arm from my shoulder, when one of the other fellows came close, and, putting his arm over my shoulder, whispered, "Father, I am a Mormon, but be careful what you say to that fellow; he is a Catholic, you can't trust him."

Putting one arm around the first fellow and one around the other, I eased them toward the road and said to them, "I am a Mormon and I am a Catholic and I am an old Presbyterian minister; you see you can both trust me. I don't think you are a Mormon and I don't think you are a Catholic, but I do think you are all three just a little bit drunk. It will soon be dark and you will be getting lost, so I think you had better be on your way."

Saluting and laughing foolishly, they replied, "All right, Father, all right," and disappeared into the gathering dusk.

With the morning, came a visitor who was a mighty contrast to those of the evening before, Herman A. Tiechert of Cokeville; a big man with a big heart; a member of the Mormon church and a son of a pioneer family. His grandmother had walked all the way from New York to the Salt Lake Valley. She had buried her mother somewhere on the trail.

His own daughter had just come home from a mission in Mexico. One son was in Germany and the youngest son, John, was leaving for a mission overseas. One could see a wistful resignation in the old rancher's face when he told us of the going of the last son from home.

On our ride this day we passed through the deserted town of Sage. We secured some water for our canteens from the construction train which stood on the side track. Then we went east through Nugget. We were now riding in a cold drizzle of rain and this place with only a filling station and a tavern or saloon looked so bedraggled and forbidding that we had no desire to stop. We rode on down the canyon a few miles farther and stopped where Fremont probably had once camped.

We had no water for the horses, but the grass was so wet that we were sure this worked no great hardship upon them. We had just enough water in our two army canteens for coffee, night and morning. With a little fire of sagebrush for cooking and to glow through the door of the tent, we were glad to rest for the night.

We were welcomed next morning by the bleating of sheep. Down the hill behind us came a flock which the master told us numbered three thousand. He invited us to fill our canteens from the wagon following in the rear. This we did, and finding a clear stream of water singing along over a bed of colored stones, we watered the horses.

We came to Kemmerer at two o'clock. We were offered the facility of the fenced-in public park as a camping place. Here was plenty of water, and grass, and a secure place to let the horses run loose. Louis Jones, the chief of police, kindly put the park at our disposal. We camped in the spot until the morning of June the fourth. Frank H. Taylor, of the Kemmerer *Gazette*, by his kindness and interest in our journey, made these two red letter days of our trek. Kemmerer's residents are historically minded, though the Old Trail did not pass through the town itself. They have a fine park, a museum, and trail markers. Here we had several pictures taken.

In coming to Kemmerer, we passed some very picturesque mountains on our left. They were vividly yellow, red and orange; rock-ribbed and seemingly ancient as the sun. We also saw the fossil beds and cliffs which, we are told, revealed some forty million years of history. Looking at them made us feel old. The morning of the fourth of June came with a bright sun, promising a fine day for our fortieth wedding anniversary. As we had set our hearts upon reaching Fort Bridger on this important date, we started early.

We followed the highway south for a short distance and were congratulating ourselves on our progess, when the sky suddenly darkened and a terrible thunder storm rolled up the valley to meet us. The lightning flashes were frequent and vivid. The huge hailstones, driven with the fury of the winds, pounded and bruised the horses until they were in an agony of pain. Once or twice, we too, in spite of our efforts to take the storm in our stride, screamed out at the pain caused by hailstones pelting our heads and shoulders.

We were mighty glad when we came to a culvert under the highway. Quickly dismounting, we sought its shelter. The horses tried to crawl in with us, and did manage to get their heads sheltered. Humped up into knots, they endured the cruelty of the storm. It was real romance for us, on our fortieth wedding anniversary, to crawl into this culvert for almost an hour, holding hands while the storm raged over us. As the sun came out, so did we, and started on.

Again that afternoon, one of those sudden storms, so common in that part of Wyoming, came volleying up the valley and again we sought cover, this time in a W.P.A. shelter camp. We were cold and uncomfortable, but there was wood and kindling in the cabin, so we soon had a warm fire going. We dried our clothes and cleaned up the cabin. In about an hour the clouds had broken and were rolling off, grumbling, toward the northeast. We took off again across the hills. The westering sun turned the blue sagebrush valley and hills into a thing of somber loveliness. The going was rather hard on the horses, as their feet would sink into the mud or slip on the soapy sides where the trail tilted, but we made several miles on the way to Bridger.

Toward sundown, over the vast stretches of sagebrush plains, we saw two flaming rainbows. We began to recite the old saw about "A rainbow in the morning is the sailor's warning, a rainbow at night is the sailor's delight," but we changed it to "A rainbow at night is the rider's delight." Riding on into the rainbow, we came to a place where water had been standing earlier in the spring but was now dry. It was an emerald jewel amid the tarnished silver of the sage. The grass was luxurious and sweet. There we pitched our tent. We called this the camp of the rainbows.

Again we were short of water. Again the horses must go without a drink. As before, we had only enough water for night and morning coffee, so, unwashed, we went to bed. Next morning, still unwashed, we took up our journey to Fort Bridger.

Unless one has spent a night alone in the desert, he will never know its strange appearance, its utter loneliness. All around, the dark purple sage; the patch of vivid green—yes, green—in the moonlight; the white tent with it's red top; the black horses, picketed and quiet; for miles not a human being, not a sound. This is nature with a sob in it's heart.

We sat by our wee fire that night with our four-point Hudson Bay blanket around both of us. When the brilliant stars came close we reached up and stole a double handful and hid them away in our hearts.

⁂

VIII

SPRINGS OF THE WESTING WATERS

We Did Not Reach Fort Bridger on our fortieth wedding anniversary. The two sudden storms and the time spent in the culvert and in the W.P.A. shelter camp, effectually wrecked our plans. We determined, however, to reach the old trading post on the fifth of June, so prepared to get our usual early start and have a day of leisurely traveling. But man proposes and Providence disposes; and Providence, in the form of three willful horses, threatened to wreck our hopes for the day.

We struck the little tent, carefully packed the panniers, and saddled up the two riding horses. Then, as there was no facility for tethering them, we threw the reins of Black Fairy over the saddle horn of Old Dynamite, at the same time dropping his loosened reins to the ground, and started to load up the Pack. As the first pannier was lifted to the pack saddle, she reared high in the air, tossing the heavy bag to the ground, and started to buck and run. This excited the saddle horses and they too started to run. It looked like one of those things, as a slang term calls it. It seemed for a few brief seconds that if we ever reached Fort Bridger it would be still another day, and on foot, but as Black Diamond flashed away I caught the end of her picket rope. After a few high leaps into the air, impelled by the tight-stretched, singing rope, I came down with my high-heeled boots digging into the desert soil. I brought her up with a round turn, then giving the rope to Mrs. Beard, I took off after the other two horses. We may have been thinking some very serious thoughts, and we may have been saying some very eloquent words. We do not clearly remember, and we have never seriously tried to recall either what we thought or what we said. We did prove that day, however, and many times since recalled, that two cannot run together unless they be agreed. Dynamite and Black Fairy were not agreed that day as to speed. The latter was a fast horse, and, woman like, was in a greater hurry. She ran ahead and across his path, causing him to circle. I cut across that circle, and, after about two hundred yards, made in less than ten seconds per hundred, I am sure, I was able to grasp his blood-flecked reins. What a grand and glorious feeling it was to get into the saddle. We came back to camp faster than we left, avoiding no sagebrush, but leaping over all. We immediately resumed our loading of the Pack.

Having finished, we sat down on the ground to relax for a few moments before mounting. We held the long, loose reins firmly in our hands lest the restive animals should make another attempt to leave us alone out there in the sagebrush. We took out a letter which we had received the day before from Quincy Scott *Oregonian* cartoonist, and read it the second time. It was most timely, as you may see for yourself. We violate no confidence when we let you read it. Here it is:

Dear John and Lulu:

I have seventeen thousand things to do this afternoon, more or less, but when I suddenly realized a few minutes ago that if I didn't get a note in the mail to you, first thing I'd know you might have completed your journey, I shoved the other things aside and here's the note. (I got your scheduled port of call from the Mt. Tabor Presbyterian Church office).

It would warm your hearts if you knew how many friends you have here in Portland, who are thinking about you and are watching for news of your progress. Among them all there are none, of course, who really know quite as well as Nell and I do how deep is the satisfaction of a jaunt like yours, as also how tough are some of the experiences that go with it. Rain, snow, gumbo, hail, lightning, skeeters, rope-burn, rattlers, quicksand, alkali, dry camp, strayed mounts—we know the whole picture and are living it over with you as you mog along day by day.

Best of luck to you, with affection from both of us.

QUINCY SCOTT

After reading the letter we felt better. We mounted and started for the fort.

The bright sunshine, the gay golden flowers, including the Indian Paint Brush with it's scarlet bonnet, soon made us forget the runaway horses. Singing as usual, we rode through Carter. We climbed the hill beyond the river and went across the sagebrush-covered plateau to Fort Bridger.

Jim Bridger must have had a flare for the aesthetic, as well as for defense and strategic trade situation, when he located his trading post here on the Black Fork of the Green River around 1837. One will travel far before he sees a bonnier spot or a more picturesque location.

As we came across the elevated plateau from the north, we could look off to the southwest and see the snow-covered Uinta

Mountains. Down below us ran the Black Fork of the Green River meadows brilliant with myriads of many-colored flowers along its banks. In the center of the landscape stood the Old Fort, with it's ancient trees standing in long lines where the officers quarters had been while it was a military establishment.

High in the air, circling with slow, graceful wing, a hawk was patrolling the reaches of the sky. Over on our right stood the white covered wagon of a sheep herder. Around it fed a vast flock, undulant as a white sea stirred by gentle winds.

We rode in single file, as the pack trains must often have come in the long ago. A great airliner skimmed effortlessly across the sky and lost itself over the valley and beyond the white Uintas. Surely this was a dream landscape, this valley of the Black Fork of the Green, with Old Fort Bridger at it's heart.

James Bridger is buried at Kansas City, Missouri. A worthy monument marks the resting place of his body, but he is not there. You cannot put the spirit beneath the sod. Jim Bridger's spirit roams the reaches of the West, forever traveling over the plains and through the mountain fastness. He was at Fort Bridger that day to welcome us. We felt his spirit with us as we came across the plateau and entered the gates to his ancient trading post. We felt him near as we stood by the grave of his half-Indian daughter, Virginia Bridger Hahn, buried there at the Old Fort.

When we arrived at Fort Bridger, the gates were thrown open for us. We spent two full and happy days, wandering over this historic place. The horses feeding in the spacious grounds, raced back and forth like wild things of the plains. At one time, in headlong flight, they leaped the fence, one after another, as sheep will often leap a tumbleweed, with each following one leaping at the same place. Fortunately for us, they found themselves in an outside pasture with a higher fence.

At our camp, from the lips of Ernest Dahlquist, member of the Historical Landmark Commission of Wyoming, we heard again the story of the fur traders, the Mountain Men, and the soldiers who guarded the territory in it's days of transition.

He told us of Bridger's first establishment—two log houses joined by a sod roof, surrounded by a high picket fence; how some fifty whites and Indians and half-breeds used to live here together; and how the place had been abandoned in 1853 on account of some trouble between Bridger and the Mormon people. He took us to see a remnant left of the old Mormon wall, relics of their own day of occupation

Close to Fort Bridger, Albert Sidney Johnston encamped with his army in November, 1857, enduring terrible hardships. Brigham Young had camped at the post in 1847 and later commissioned Orson Hyde to establish Fort Supply only nine miles away on Willow Creek. In June, 1858, Johnston took possession of the trading post and built a military establishment which was maintained until 1890. The ill-fated Donner party had camped at the post in 1846.

When we found the original Pony Express stables so well preserved, with box stalls still intact, tying rings still in place, and much of the planking in the stalls as when first put down, we almost expected to see the rider come thundering up with sparks flashing from the horses' hoofs; to see the relay change and to hear the hoof-beats die away in the distance.

In one corner of these storied grounds we found a monument erected to an old stable dog, one who had been a favorite of everyone around the fort in his day. On the stone were carved the words:

> THORNBURG DIED IN 1888,
> *Man never had a better, truer, braver, friend.*
> *Sleep on, old fellow, across the range.*

As we left Fort Bridger, going out through the narrow gate, Old Dynamite began to buck and hit one side of the gate, knocking off a stone. Black Diamond also became greatly excited and smashed against the other gate post, knocking off some of the stones. I fear we did more damage to the gate than several years of natural attrition would have done. However, with many a Good Luck ringing in our ears, we took off along the trail for the Spring of the Westing Waters. We headed now north-northeast for Pacific Springs on the Old South Pass.

We watered the horses that day just beyond the monument, where it is recorded that the Mormons had passed in July,

1847. Two bridges here cross the Black Fork. We stopped at the first, a wooden structure.

We went on up the trail and over the road to the Church Buttes, a formation looking wonderfully like some domed mosque or cathederal. Truly this blue and black sandstone hill, rising almost a hundred feet upon it's base, has been appropriately named.

This day we saw our first antelope, two of them, bounding along the darkling prairie, with their white flags twinkling fitfully as they disappeared over the hill. We were to see hundreds of these graceful creatures before we were through the stretches of Wyoming. All day we rode through what seemed like the bed of some ancient lake, showing where the pre-historic waters had boiled and surged around the jutting headlands.

We camped twenty-eight miles from Fort Bridger, not far from Granger. We had very little grass but we gave the horses a double portion of oats, threw our sleeping bags down on the sand, and pondered the vast loneliness of the Wyoming plains. We were quite short of water again this night. We understood why the Indians who camp out sometimes have dirty faces.

At Granger, which in the old sheep and cattle days had known a somewhat gay and boisterous life, we found the well-preserved building of the Stage Coach and Pony Express station. This was another of the ghost towns of the West. Here we had trouble getting information about the trail to the crossing of the Green. Inquiring at the two stores, we were told that only a Roy Adams, the tavern keeper, knew anything about the trail, but that he knew everything about it, as he had lived in Granger all of his life, and had hunted over every part of the desert country. Off to the tavern we went. I had a good laugh at myself, an old Presbyterian minister, hunting up a tavern. It was closed and it is the only time in my life that I ever felt sorry for a closed tavern.

We did not know just what to do, so sat on the weather-beaten step to think. Soon around the corner of the building came a most likeable looking man and we asked him if he owned the institution. He said that he did, and putting his key into the lock, opened the door, and invited us in. Stepping around a rather shabby looking box or bar, he said, "What will you have?"

Before I could tell him that I just wanted information, another old fellow, who seemed to have lived for years in the desert, came in. His hair was long and uncombed. His beard, stained with tobacco, was white and somewhat tangled. His worn and patched Levis were tucked down in the tops of his boots. Looking me over, he asked me to have a drink. When I refused, as courteously as I knew how, he looked at me in a rather cold, hard way, and in a matter-of-fact voice said, "Well, what in Hell did you come in here for?" When I told him just to get some information about the Old Trail to the South Pass, he seemed mollified and said, "Well, if anybody can tell you, he can."

The barkeeper then took a pencil and drew me a map of the Trail, putting in all the information needed; in fact, the best bit of direction that had been given anywhere along the journey. Then he said, "Now, you will find it rather difficult to get on the right track, for up here some two or three miles there are several trails winding back and forth and the right one will be hard to find. I will take you in the pick-up, show you where the Old Trail starts, and bring you back. The Missus can stay here with the horses until we return." So locking the door, he took the truck and we started off.

Looking back, I saw that Mrs. Beard had sat down on the shabby old steps. She was holding all three horses and looked a rather forlorn, little creature, not too happy about it all. I could not help laughing, though, to think of her, a minister's wife, keeping bar out there in the sagebrush country of Wyoming. I well knew that she would be equal to any occasion. Without any misgivings, I went with the tavern keeper to reconnoiter the trail. We were not long gone and we had not stopped the car when she was in the saddle, ready to resume the ride. Without difficulty, we came to what our informant had said was the Big Island Crossing of the Green. This crossing had been a difficult hurdle for the old travelers to make.

We camped on the south side of the river, not far from a little red cabin, a shelter built by the W.P.A., and next morning crossed the river and headed due north for the Sandy, another of the obstacles which had been difficult in the early years. On this day's travel we failed to follow instructions and got down to where the Sandy empties into the Green. We had erred too far to the west, but had done this deliberately, rather than toward the east, for we were anxious to avoid the Bad Lands, which lay on our right. On reaching the Sandy we turned right and followed up ten or twelve miles to a bridge crossing.

On the ride up to the bridge, we met a party of surveyors at work, whose first question was, "How are you fixed for water?" We told them not too well. The ride this day had been hard and hot and we had almost emptied our canteens, thinking that when we reached the Sandy we could drink its water. The government men told us that it would be all right for the horses, but not for us. Too much running over irrigated fields above and too much alkali, they said.

They asked us where we intended to stop for the night, and when we told them at the bridge, and that we planned to break camp the next morning at nine o'clock, they took a big Forest Service canteen and gave it to us. "This will be plenty for your cooking tonight and for breakfast in the morning. At nine o'clock we will be back from Kemmerer and bring you fresh water for tomorrow's ride."

We thanked them with such gratitude as only he knows who has had lips cracked and throat parched from riding through a thirsty land, and rode on up the river. We crossed the Sandy over the bridge and went into camp on the north shore. We were some twenty miles out in the desert, alone, but supremely contented.

We had crossed the historic Sandy! We were happy! The horses were happy with an abundance of grass. They drank thirstily, kneeling down like wild creatures. Good old range horses! The desert was becoming our own familiar home.

We changed our evening meal to canned corned beef and tomatoes, with bread cooked in them. After supper we had a cold plunge in the river, then with a cozy fire at our feet, and the blanket over our shoulders, we watched the sun go down among broken clouds. We marvelled at the changing panorama of cloud forms.

How peacefully the river flowed that night. All along it's banks the grass was green, and flowers were sending up their sweet perfume. Many cattle, stately bulls, fond mothers, and playful calves were finding a full life from it's bounty.

We were deliberate about breaking camp the next morning, for we were not to leave this spot until nine o'clock, about an hour later than our usual start. The horses seemed quite ready for their morning's oats, as they reminded us with repeated whinnies. For some reason or other they were reconciled to the saddling and loading operations and gave us little trouble. When nine o'clock came—and on the minute the Government men with ice water for our canteens, they stepped out at our bidding with long, eager strides on their way to Pacific Springs.

This day we saw many antelope. Once seven of them came up the trail to meet us. They ran alongside for some distance, then, crossing in front of us, paralleled our path again, as though challenging us to a race. Finally they turned, and with the speed of thought, vanished over the hills.

It was hot going, but when clouds passed over the sun, we took off our hats and rode gratefully in the shadows as long as they lasted. The emigrant found hard traveling along this waterless stretch of the trail. We appreciated some of the depressing conditions which they had found.

There is a fine trail marker at Farson. Here Jim Bridger and Brigham Young met and argued concerning the fertility of the soil around what is now Salt Lake City. Young seems to have had the best of the argument, as well as a greater store of prophetic insight.

Crossing a bridge four or five miles out of Farson, our horses became badly frightened when a group of loose horses flashed out from under. Black Fairy almost got away on a mad run. When we got them settled down, we were pretty well shaken up and decided to camp. Immediately across the bridge, we pitched the tent alongside a wire fence. That night we had another rain with a terrifying display of lightning, but, with the down bags snugly pulled around us, we challenged the elements to do their worst, and went to sleep happy in the thought that tomorrow night we would camp at the Pacific Springs.

The meadowlarks had been singing for a full hour before we got out of our sleeping bags at five o'clock. We secured seventy pounds of new, clean oats from a rancher, who asked us how much we had been paying for them. We told him sometimes four cents a pound and sometimes five. "Well," he said, "I will charge you three."

The old South Pass is a place of storied romance. The old South Pass. That name thrilled through the days of the early migration. Often they tried to picture what it would be like. Most of them, uninformed of course, expected to see a narrow gap high up between rough and rugged mountains, reached by laborious, dangerous going alongside deep canyons. Little did they realize that through all which is now western Nebraska and Wyoming, they were climbing by rather easy grade up to the crest, an altitude of about 7,560 feet. The pass itself was some twenty miles wide with the big Wind River Range far away to the west and north, and with great headlands of the Oregon Buttes to the west and south. This pass, covered with it's growth of silvery sage, could well have been a parcel lifted out of the home-land which they had left behind. So gradual had been the ascent and so gentle would be the descent they would never know just where that invisible line of the Continental Divide actually ran. Only when they found waters running west did they realize that home was now indeed far behind. They had crossed over the line and were now in the Oregon country, and God had, in very fact, smoothed down a way for His wagon trains.

Of course, the Indians knew of this easy route into the West but evidently were not eager to make it known. Lewis and Clark probably heard of a pass lying there to the south of their route to the Pacific Ocean in 1805. Several different men have been credited with it's discovery. On the monument that marks his resting place in Kansas City, Missouri, Jim Bridger is given the honor of it's discovery and the time as 1827. Altrocchi tells us that Ezekiel Williams attempted to reach California by way of the South Pass in 1807, and that he died near the springs or headwaters of the North Platte. Crooks and Stuart, the returning Astorians, probably passed along its northern rim in 1812. Some give the honor to one Entienne Provost, one of

Ashley's men, and the time, 1823, and others say it was Jedediah Smith and Thomas Fitzpatrick of the same Ashley expedition, and the time as 1824. We know, of course, that B. L. E. Bonneville took some twenty wagons through the Pass in 1832, and that John C. Fremont went through in 1842. Fitzpatrick had already guided the Bidwell Bartleson party through in 1841.

We will probably never know who was the actual discoverer. And it little matters who found it, for it was there and was well known when the flood of western travelers needed a way to get through the mighty barriers of the mountains. We knew that not one of the men who passed over it had been more eager to see it than were we. Tonight, we would reach it.

Today we passed about a quarter of a mile of the Old Trail, which the Government had fenced in with wire, in order to preserve the old ruts. Late in the afternoon we topped a hill and looked down on a narrow strip of green, running for about a mile through a shallow ravine. Down it's center was a thread of crystal clear water. On the right loomed the vast bulk of the Oregon Buttes, and, far away to the left, the Wind River Mountains reared their towering snow-covered peaks. We were looking down upon that little silver thread of water which flowed westward from Pacific Springs.

All day long the sun beat down upon our backs. We were hot and uncomfortable. Our eyes were drawn almost together from squinting at the sun-splashed sage. We were dusty and tired from the saddles, but now we felt and knew what the prophet meant when he said, "As the hart panteth after the water brooks." We think we knew what the men on the trail felt when they found the clear, cold spring whose waters ran to the western seas.

On July 4, 1836, Narcissa Whitman and Eliza Spalding crossed over the crest of Old South Pass above the spring, and, coming on down, knelt by it's waters and put their parched lips to it's cooling stream.

It is said that when the emigrants reached the summit of the Pass and knew that they were drinking of waters that emptied into the Pacific, some of them danced, some sang, some wept, and some seemed to go insane. We can well believe this.

Back of them lay the land that most of them would never see again. Before them lay long miles of terrible danger, herculean labor, and strange adventure.

Ours was only joy and gladness that night, when we camped near the summit and drank long and deeply of the "Spring of the Westing Waters."

IX

GOOSE EGG

Our next objective was Goose Egg. Before the start of this ride, two Government men, who were camped at the springs took us for a ride of some hundred miles or more in a circle to the Sweetwater River and down through Atlantic City, famous in the gold digging days, but now a sad old ghost town with its glory forever departed. From Atlantic City and it's huge ridge of washed-out placer gravel we went down the darkling gulch to South Pass City, a town that also was once quite famous. Now only a general store, a saloon, and an old jail remain, all full of ghosts of yesterday. One would like to get into that tumble-down jail to hunt out the relics that completely fill all it's space.

South Pass Ctiy, founded in 1849, was the capital of vast territories, according to the story told us by an old-timer whom we met in the saloon, where we went seeking information about this part of the country. He volunteered the information that South Pass once boasted a population of some five thousand souls, among them was a famous suffragette, whose name he had forgotten.

Next day at the springs we had a real fright when Black Fairy, venturing too far out toward the stream, suddenly sank almost out of sight in a bog hole. It was only after mighty efforts of her stout little heart that she released herself from the sucking grip of the mud and got safely back to solid ground. She was a sorry-looking sight. It took hours to get her cleaned up.

The woman of our party, about this time, was doing out a washing. And the male member spent the rest of the day inspecting some of the old structures standing near the camp. They were built of logs and had stood there for seventy-five years. The barn had twenty-five stalls; the shed at it's side would have accommodated twenty-five more horses. There was a blacksmith shop and the relics of a saloon and in which, it is said, several men were killed. One large log cabin was still usable. Yesterday was with us this day here at the springs.

In the evening we visited with the Government Wild Life men, Delbert Cram and Robert Patterson. One of them asked, "Chaplain, if you were going fishing and could have your choice of two flies and two only, which ones would you choose?"

Unhesitatingly, I replied, "A Royal Coachman Bucktail and a Gray Hackle."

"Well, here they are and here is a seven-foot tapered leader and here is a line. If you should get off the trail and get lost before you reach Sweetwater, you might need to catch some fish. When you do arrive, you will be able to cut a rod from the willows that grow along the bank. Remember, the Oregon Buttes are on your right rear, the Wind River Mountains at your left rear. Keep going north and east and you will make it. You, of course, have a compass?"

With the horses now fresh, with plenty of oats in the panniers, with our own supplies fully replenished from the general store of South Pass City, and with the fishing tackle securely packed away in the saddle bags, we felt equal to the trail; even to being lost for several days, in case that should happen, as we covered vast, empty space between us and the Sweetwater.

At nine o'clock we said goodbye to our friends, mounted the ponies and were off for the rest of the journey through the Old South Pass and on our way to Goose Egg. We rode on up the old Emigrant Trail until we came to the Oregon Trail marker placed there by Ezra Meeker and to the marker erected to commemorate the fact that Narcissa Whitman and Eliza

Spalding had stood at this place on July 4, 1836, the first white women ever to cross the divide.

We dismounted to read the inscription. With heads uncovered, we stood there amidst the vast loneliness of the sage-covered pass, and our minds and hearts went back across the more than a hundred years to that night of February 18, 1836, when Narcissa was married in the Presbyterian Church of Angelica, New York. We recalled that, when the final hymn of the service was sung, Narcissa alone sang the last verse. By then tears so filled the eyes and sobs so filled the breasts of the congregation that they could not finish the song. But the brave, golden-haired Narcissa, with a clear golden voice, sang the song through to the end. Then, taking her young husband by the hand, they turned their faces toward the sunset and rode away into the West. They came out on what was later known as this Old Oregon Trail, and had stood here on July 4, 1836. Here again, upon their knees, they rededicated their lives to the winning of the West and the souls of it's people to God.

As we stood before these stones at the summit of the pass, we were suddenly impressed with the vastness, the emptiness, the lonesomeness of this Wyoming land. Often we would turn and look back and again we would look toward the Oregon Buttes, which seemed to be forever near us on our right and again lift our eyes to the great Wind River range on our left. Somehow, the mountains and hills seemed more friendly and companionable than the vast reaches of the sagebrush plains that lay ahead.

All through the ride over the pass, we saw literally hordes of antelope. They would appear and disappear in every direction. Sometimes it seemed uncanny to pass over a hill, turn and look back to see one of these strange creatures gazing at us as if he had been watching us all the time.

About noon we came to a sheepherder's camp. The old Indian herder invited us to go to his wagon to have dinner but we were soon anxious to reach the Sweetwater by night that we declined and ate our lunch as we rode along. He accompanied us for several miles. He was a member of the Catholic Church. He told us how one of the Catholic Sisterhoods had cared for his three little children when his wife passed away some six years before. There was something wistful in his face when, pointing out the way our trail went, he turned to take his own trail back to his lonesome camp. We now wished we had taken time to eat dinner with him in his wagon home.

Just a little later, we passed the historic Burnt Ranch Pony Express Station and near sundown reached the Sweetwater where we had planned to camp. Feverishly, we unsaddled, picketed out the horses, drove down the four pegs of the tent, and went fishing. Mrs. Beard volunteering to gather the wood for the fire and to dig the hole for the grill, sent me hopefully to the river with the statement that she expected fish, and would render just enough bacon to fry them in and would have the frying pan hot and ready to receive them, and, flourishing the long-handled frying pan like an Indian war club, she proclaimed, "You better bring some back."

Within a half hour I returned with five as lovely trout as the eyes of any Isaac Walton ever saw. We had trout for supper that night and for breakfast next morning. We had not gotten lost in the Bad Lands either, but we surely needed the fish, and we had fished the flies tandem.

The next morning we rode east-by-north along the south-side of the Sweetwater. On this day we began to experience the real trouble caused by flies. They were little black things that would come up under the front of the horses, enter their nostrils, and simply drive them crazy. Rearing, they would strike at the flies and again would try to avoid them by springing to one side or the other. A rider had to do a real job in order to stay in the saddle. The effort was truly exhausting. The trouble always increased as we neared a sheep camp. We finally learned to carry a branch of some leafy shrub, which we continually waved about the heads of the horses and so drove off the pests.

Down the trail by a sheep camp, we came upon a stone marking the grave of a young girl, one of an emigrant train, who had died of bacon colic, whatever that might be. Just over a little hillock was the grave of a Union soldier, who had been identified when his grave was first found by some remnant that remained of the old blue uniform and by some brass buttons. The skull had been split.He probably had been killed while sleeping. There were many tragedies on the trail in the old days.

The mistress of the sheep camp claimed to be the only woman flock tender in the State of Wyoming. A well-read woman, she had the story of the winning of the West by heart. She had also heard of our ride over the trail and had been watching for our coming. She cordially invited us to camp with her but the flies were so annoying that we decided to push on down the trail and try to make the bridge over the Sweetwater by night.

Soon we became confused, being unable to see the Oregon Buttes or the Wind River Mountains that had been our fixed points. It was about noon and we lost our sense of direction, but learning through the years never to doubt the compass, we dismounted, put down the old Stetson hat, leveled the compass on it's crown, and, allowing for the magnetic variation, we found true north and started in that direction for the river.

We hit the bridge right on the nose but found it barricaded in order to separate two flocks of sheep. What to do? Well, if we could not cross on the bridge we could ford the river. We had learned from the pioneers that he who stops at any obstacle will not get far on his way. So into the river we rode. It was fun and the horses enjoyed it. Coming up out of the stream we found the wagon of a young sheep herder. He was standing on the doubletree watching us, but as soon as he saw that we were going to visit him, he ran like a squirrel down the wagon tongue to meet us and, holding out his hand, announced, "Coffee, coffee."

I replied, "No, Lad, it is getting late and we must be on our way. We have to find a good place to make camp and it takes time."

In a soft, liquid voice he repeated, "Make camp, take time." Then shaking his head, for he could not understand what I said, he apologetically explained, "Spanish," and, passing his hand against his breast, he again repeated, "Make camp, take time, coffee, coffee?"

I was just about to ride on when the other party of this trail-riding adventure objected, "Chaplain, he wants us to have a cup of coffee with him. We can make camp in the dark if necessary, or spend this night without a camp. Let's accept the boy's invitation, what do you say?"

"O.K." I agreed, and before I could finish the sentence, she was off the horse and running up the tongue of the wagon as gracefully as the Spanish lad had come down. By the time I had tethered the horses to a wagon wheel, she had a tortilla in one hand and a cup of coffee in the other, and the lad with a gracious and friendly smile, was holding out a cup of coffee to me. I do not remember a more delicious lunch than that piece of scone or bannock or tortilla, call it what you wish, hot and dripping with melted butter, and that cup of strong, black coffee.

When ready to go, I slipped my arm around the shoulder of the boy, probably eighteen or nineteen years old, just a boy to me, and said to him, "Lad, do you get lonesome out here caring for your sheep?"

"Lonesome, lonesome, lonesome," he murmured, trying to get the meaning. Then he gave up the attempt, and again putting his hand on his breast repeated, "Spanish, Spanish."

As we rode away we looked back and saw him standing at the door of his wagon, tall, slim, with the setting sun playing around his bonny, curly head, his white teeth showing through his red lips, and we seemed to hear him saying, "Spanish, coffee, coffee." Like ships that pass in the night, and speak each other in passing, so we met and passed in the gloaming of a Wyoming evening.

We turned east and rode along the north shore of the river for some miles, then pitched our camp not ten feet from it's bank. Here was abundance of grass, the horses could drink from the river, and the tent was sheltered by the willows from the strong wind that was now blowing. Just across the stream the green meadow was a riot of color, sown broadcast with purple iris and yellow flowers. We named this our "Dream Camp". The odor of the sweet-smelling mint that made the spot so delightful will be remembered for many a day.

Next morning as we rode along the narrow ledge between the river and the hills, the odor of mint gave way to the perfume of the wild rose, which filled the air with it's fragrance. We had extreme difficulty on that narrow pass getting by a shepherd's wagon which we met upon the road. Horse nature is sometimes hard to understand. We had seen and passed many a sheepherder's wagon both standing still and rolling and the horses had never seemed especially concerned, but you would have thought the Devil himself was driving this man's wagon, for, as often as we came up to it, the horses would plunge wildly, wheel, and start on a run in the opposite direction. We finally rode back a short way, turned their heads into a sort of recess in the hill and let the wagon drive by. When it had passed we rode through the entire flock of sheep with no difficulty whatever.

We went through miles of sweet clover, the yellow blossoms reaching to the horses' knees. We passed through the ice sloughs, of which many of the emigrants speak in their diaries. We were told that even today it is possible to dig down and find ice. It is also told that there are more bones of cattle in that slough today than there are cattle in Wyoming. We also heard that much equipment had sunk out of sight when men had tried to drain some part of it. True or false, it is a good story.

We came to "The Home on the Range", a filling station with some few tourist cabins along the road. Samuel Peterson and his wife had taken up a homestead here and had started their rather humble business. They insisted that we put the horses in the pasture and spend the night, at their expense, in one of the cabins. However, we loved the little tent, which had now so long been our home, so we declined. We pitched it in the pasture, but ate breakfast with these delightful people. He was an old Alaska man, who knew how to make sour dough pancakes. It is worth a drive, half across the continent, just to get a breakfast of these cakes. Some day we intend to take the Buick and go back for a batch. Sour dough pancakes, melted butter, honey—man, man, man! a breakfast for the Gods or, better yet, for the Riders of the Trail.

The memory of the sour dough cakes, however, can not blot out the memory of that night spent in the small, wire enclosed pasture. Inside our tent, with its bobbinet door zipped up tight, we could lie and laugh at the battalion after battalion, regiment, brigade, divisions, army corps of mosquitoes—Satan's devilish imps—that battered themselves against the tent. So thick they came that the tent door became a thick, black blanket which almost shut out the air. Inside we could laugh at their ineffectual, devilish songs but outside they made life a living hell for the horses. All night long the animals would lie down and roll, then get up and walk and trot, and then madly race around and around the enclosure. Sometimes they would make sounds like the voices of humans in distress.

This camp at "The Home on the Range" we renamed "The Camp of the Devils." It is near the Three Crossings of the Sweetwater. When morning came the mosquitoes, now augmented with flies, were so bad that we could not feed the horses their usual breakfast of oats. With great difficulty we got them saddled and the panniers on the Pack. Then Mr. Peterson led them around while we ate breakfast.

We were truly happy when one of the frequent Wyoming storms overtook us, for riding in the rain and dodging hail stones is far better than fighting flies and mosquitoes.

Once more at McGrew, Nebraska, we were to encounter these pests of the prairies and on that night, all night long, we sat up and kept a smoke going to free the horses from their tormentors.

At Fort Laramie, we had not only the mosquitoes but swarms of little white gnats, so thick, that passing my hand down over the breasts of the horses, I would find them actually dripping with blood. Next morning the place where we picketed the horses at Fort Laramie looked like the rings of a circus, for all night long the horses had raced in a circle at the ends of their picket ropes.

That noon we ate lunch with J. L. McIntosh at the Split Rock Ranch. We took off the saddles and the panniers to give the horses a change, never previously removed at noon, but the horses had spent such a hard, restless night that they needed this added relief. When we saddled up again, we tried to pay the owner of the ranch but he refused to take any money, saying it was a custom as old as the ranch that a visitor on foot or horseback was always fed and bedded down at night, without charge. When we departed, he filled a sack with oats for the horses.

We now took off again on the actual Old Trail and followed it through meadows and over hills covered with yellow cactus blooms and thistles turning into delicate pink and tall lovely blue flowers that looked like delphiniums. We passed by the foundations of what had been an old stage coach station and camped at the big, white, empty house on the Turkey Track Ranch. We had passed over Rattle Snake Flat and by Whiskey Point, places very famous in the early days.

The Turkey Track Ranch was owned by Mr. Sun, whose home ranch, further along the trail we reached the next day. We spent some hours at this place, looking over the large collection of historic things gathered in the private museum. The ranch itself is the perfect picture of what we always thought a western cow ranch should be. It is situated near the famous Devil's Gate.

We did not stay at the ranch that night, for we wanted to get to Independence Rock and camp there. We passed some graves of old pioneers and camped on the bank of the Sweetwater. We wanted to camp close against the rock but several belligerent white-faced Hereford bulls on the spot made their displeasure known by warning bellows. We thought discretion to be the better part of valor and camped down near the bridge by the river.

That evening the Suns came up to see us. They brought some corn for the horses, some jars of cold milk, a roll of butter, some fresh eggs, and loaf of home-made bread. After supper they took us in their car up around the Rock to the Old Stage Coach Station that had been burned by the Indians. He also showed us the crossing of the Sweetwater and the remains of the foundations of a bridge that had spanned the river at this place.

How we longed to linger here until we could have read every name cut into this old rock. What flood-tides of people passed by here, camped here, cut their names into its granite. Stuart and Crooks, of the Astorians, camped here and named this granite monument. Fremont painted or carved a great cross on the Rock on August 23, 1842. This has disappeared.

Here close up against this famous landmark, William Barlow, who came out in 1845, followed the suggestion of Jason Lee and threw away a small fortune, when he left behind a three-hundred pound box of the finest grafted apple seedlings, which he had brought all the way from Illinois.

By the side of the great rock are the graves of two little children. No one knows their names. Securely they rest beneath the shelter of it's eternal strength.

Leaving the Rock behind, we rode all day up and down the hills (mostly up, it seems) to come to the crest of the rise. A dream view opened before us. There were the Red Buttes with their long, crimson ridges like corridors down to the deep, blue waters of a lake, dammed in among the red hills. Beyond that were deep canyons filled with such blue as we find only in nature and in Parish pictures.

Going down the long road, we found a mighty fortress which nature had built with the red, red rocks. We seemed to descend into an unbelievable world of wonder. What would I not give for the power to describe it? Riding on, we came to a little settlement at the bottom of a long declivity, two or three houses, and a store and post office combined.

As we approached the store to get some needed supplies, a dainty little woman, Mrs. Zola Zorbaugh, came to the door and said, "We know who you are. We have been watching you come down the trail. We have some hot coffee ready and waiting; will you not come in?"

We had been riding all day with blue flowers all around us. And here, at the end of the day, we had reached the Blue Flower of the traveler's dream, rest, peace, refreshment, hospitality. Would to God we could build a whole world where every traveler along it's lonesome trail could find such welcome and such hospitality. We sat there and rested for awhile, thoroughly enjoying our visit with this friendly little spirit of the hills, then rode on to camp that night on the east-going Platte. It's very name made us feel at home.

The next day was Sunday. Up to this time we had rested on the Sabbath day. Another old fellow talking to us about this resting on the seventh day had also exclaimed, "I suppose if you were to ride on Sunday, the horses' shoes would grow so hot they would set the prairies on fire."

Well, at any rate, we had not previously ridden on Sunday, but this Sabbath we rode half a day. The shoes on the horses were getting thin again; in fact, the Pack had worn one of her shoes entirely through and had lost one half of it. Our oats were gone and we wanted to get to Casper, Wyoming, where we hoped to be able to secure a new supply before the horses would miss too many meals. We set no prairie fires along the way, but we did find some pleasant experiences, and some otherwise.

This day we passed the Bessemer Bend in the river, near which Stuart had built his cabin on his return east in November, 1812. We came in sight of more of the gorgeous Red Buttes.

We met a man who stopped his jeep and asked us if there was anything he could do for us to help us on our way. There was something quite striking in this man and his jeep and we readily stopped for a visit.

His was one of the regular Army jeeps. In it he had two fine looking hounds. He was a man well over six feet tall, without an ounce of superfluous flesh on his body, straight as an arrow, broadshouldered, and with a step as smooth and supple as an Indian's. His face was lean and brown like well-tanned leather, his eyes were blue, scintillating but kindly. As he stepped from his jeep, came over and patted old Dynamite on the neck, and then reached up to shake hands, I instinctively felt, and thought to myself, he is the kind of a man I should like to have behind me in a real hot or desperate fight.

We visited for awhile, then he said, "Well, Father, is there anything I can do for you?"

"Nothing," I said, "unless you can tell me if there is any place along the way where I can secure oats for my horses to-night."

He replied, "I do not think you could buy feed short of Casper."

"Well, that is just too bad," I said, "that is too far for the horses to travel, so we must try to find a camping place where there is plenty of grass."

"That too, will be hard to find," he said. Then he inquired, "Where do you intend to camp?"

"Looking at my watch, I replied, "We will ride for about an hour, some four or five miles, on up the trail."

"That will be at Goose Egg," said he. "Come to think about it, you might be able to find a pretty good camping place there. Good-by again and good luck." Getting into his jeep he rode off.

"Do you know, I like that fellow," I said to Mrs. Beard.

"I do too," she replied.

Then we too started on up the way toward Goose Egg.

Just before sunset we topped a ridge and looked down upon Goose Egg. It is just a post office on the highway and it is named after the ranch made famous in the story of *The Virginian* by Owen Wister. At this place the Virginian, with the help of the other cowboys, scrambled the babies. Later in the day we visited the famous old ranch house, now rapidly falling into ruins.

Going into the post office, we asked permission to picket the horses in a pasture that cornered at this place, and the postmaster asked, "Why don't you picket them down there in that little park?"

"Well, it would be dandy to do that," I replied, "but someone might object."

"Oh, I reckon not," the postmaster rejoined, "it belongs to me."

"O. K.," we joyfully said and, turning about, we proceeded to make camp down in that little green cup in the hills — an ideal place. A clear stream of water ran across the ground and the grass was abundant. We were all well set, even if, for once, there was no oats for the horses.

A small shepherd lad rode down into the camping ground with us, and, dismounting, said, "Mister," would you care if I helped you unsaddle the horses?" He unsaddled the Black Fairy and assisted me in unpacking the panniers, all the time patting the horses with admiring hands and asking every conceivable question about our journey. When all the little duties were done and the camp duly set up, he said, "Well, good-by now, I must be going," and, mounting his shaggy pony, he rode away. In about fifteen minutes, he returned with a quart of oats in a sack. Handing them to me, he said, "I thought, Mister, the horses might enjoy a feed of oats after their long journey." Again he mounted and rode off into the gathering twilight. I have often thought since, that little handful of oats was dust of gold from his heart of love for all created things.

He had barely left, when a jeep came careening down to the little park and our friend of the afternoon stepped out, lifted a hundred-pound sack of oats from the car and threw them down, saying, "These will last you to Casper and beyond." The horses had a double feed that night. This government trapper had driven clear to Casper to get the oats for us; he said he could not bear the thought of horses going hungry.

We fed the horses, then sat down on a log in front of the fire and swapped stories of the West. Bill had many to tell. As he left, he looked at me and said, "Well, Mr. Beard, I like you."

I looked at him and said, "And I like you, what is your name?"

He replied, "Bill Farnsworth, but just call me Bill."

I said, "And mine is Beard, Chaplain Beard, but just call me John."

"All right, that's a go," he said, "I hope we meet again, if not here, then up there."

"If not here, then over there, across the range," I said.

"Good-by, Bill." "Good-by, John," and the jeep disappeared into the night.

X

CAMP OF THE RATTLESNAKES

Next day, we rode through the Battlefield of the Red Buttes to the place, near the Platte bridge, where young Caspar W. Collins had been needlessly sent to his death, in an Indian war. It is said that between four and five thousand people had lost their lives along the Trail we were traveling from the South Pass to Fort Laramie before

1867. Perhaps no death was so unnecessary as that of the young Lieutenant Collins, for whom the city of Casper is named. On July 26, 1865, the lieutenant and his men, through the vicious, blundering folly of one somewhat higher in command, were entirely wiped out by an overwhelming band of painted savages. One wishing to know the heroism of this young officer and the pathos of his untimely death should read the booklet *Fort Caspar: Platte Bridge Station*, by Alfred James Mokler.

Ours was a very busy, but most enjoyable time spent with the friendly optimistic people of Casper. When we entered the city, we were met and entertained by the Casper Riding Club, the Chamber of Commerce, the editor of the *Caspar Tribune*, Mr. E. E. Hanway. Mr. Clarence Gould, of the J. C. Penny Company, presented Mrs. Beard with a fringed leather coat, which perfectly completed her Western riding habit. (I married Mr. and Mrs. Gould twenty-five years ago.) We spent three hours at breakfast with Mr. and Mrs. T. S. Foster, elder in the Presbyterian Church, then went out to see the Fort, now restored, which is situated close to the old bridge site of the Mormon Crossing. We made arrangements to have the horses all shod; talked to the men of the Rotary Club, and in the evening to the Lion's Club; bought a new hat for Mrs. Beard, broadcast an interview over K. V. O. C.; then rested in our white tent, which was pitched on the green lawn of the radio station.

When we rode away on Thursday morning, June 24, we were escorted for five miles by Romie Nunn, president of the Riding Club, and Tom Connolly, on his golden palomino stallion. When we parted, I threw my rainbow-hued scarf over Connolly's neck. I had learned to love that Irish lad, both on account of his skill in shoeing my horses, and for his love of his old Irish mother, and I wanted to give him something as a remembrance. This little act of friendliness almost caused both of us to be policed by our horses; for when he came near enough for me to put the scarf around his neck, his big golden palomino and my big Dynamite pulled a real Donny Brook and began to fight like the true demons they were. Both Tom and I pulled leather before we got the horses separated and quieted down, Then, with a good-bye and good luck we parted.

Life is made up of meetings and partings.

This day we rode mile after mile through the throbbing, pulsing heart of the great oil field that centers in the vicinity of Casper, and camped at Glenrock, at the very edge of the historic rock of the emigrants.

Most appetizing and delicious was the lunch of chili and other dainties put into our saddle bags by Otto Bennett, the Chili King of Casper. We ate this lunch standing, huddled with the horses in an angry, driving rain, which was mixed with sleet and hail. Hot chili is great food for a cold day.

As we came into Glenrock, C. W. Hershey of the Conoco Oil Company came out and invited us to camp in their little park. The oil company has created a neat gem in this park along the way. There was a strip of green grass on which to pitch our tent, sheltering shade under which we could rest, a stove and a table, and pure, fresh water for our cooking. Back of it was a pasture in which we were invited to turn the horses. Here was a real public service.

Through this oil-producing country, the pioneers had gone, utterly unconscious of the wealth that lay beneath their feet, but they had been mindful of the beauty which God had woven in its natural beauty. The name they gave to this camping spot, Glenrock, reveals their appreciation of all lovely things and the poetry and music in their own souls.

Next morning, we were sent happily on our way by N. O. Reed, editor of the Glenrock newspaper, who had come out to wish us God Speed.

We soon passed by the home of "Desert Dust", the famous wild Palomino stallion of the mountains, and came to Douglas, the "Mile High City." Several miles before reaching the town, we were met by three state policemen, who took our pictures, but not our fingerprints and told us of the fine facilities awaiting for our evening camp at the fair grounds. Three miles out, we were met by a newspaper man, who likewise photographed us and who also told us of the fair grounds. We were happy to think that we would not have to give too much anxious care about a place to camp. But such was not to be the case.

As we came down into Douglas, we were invited into the cafe for a cup of coffee. Here we experienced the true spirit of

TRAIL MARKER, KEMMERER, WYOMING

GOOSE EGG RANCH, WYOMING.
It was here that the babies were scrambled in Owen Wister's
book, *The Virginian*

THE GUARD HOUSE, OLD FORT LARAMIE, WYOMING

THE GHOST TOWN OF FAMOUS OLD SOUTH PASS CITY,
NEBRASKA

western hospitality and the true heart of the people of this mile-high city. We met a rancher, Roy Combs, who had an enclosed pasture of fifteen or twenty acres and who graciously informed us that it was ours for as long as we wished to stay.

This meeting with Mr. Combs seemed almost providential, for, while drinking our coffee in the cafe, the old Pack had lain down, rolled over, and torn the panniers loose. By the time we got this fixed up, it was dark, but we started for the fair grounds, happy in the thought that we could easily make camp. Riding up to the keeper's house, we asked to see the man in authority. We were informed that the Joe Louis fight was on, and that he could not be disturbed by visitors until it was finished. With a chuckle at the importance of a good prize-fight, we rode on past, and camped in the pasture of the generous rancher, Roy Combs.

We were also laughing at another incident that had occurred in the cafe. We were all sitting on high stools and drinking our coffee from the common counter. The place was full of people. All seemed most interested in the story of our ride. They were asking questions about the distance we had come and how far we yet had to go. When Mrs. Beard mentioned the fact that we were to end the journey at Independence, Missouri, an old fellow, dressed in the costume of the hills, stepped over, put a silver dollar on the counter, pushed it under her hand, saying, "There, woman, you are going to need this before you get there," and then turned and walked out.

It rained again that night. Joe Louis won. Next morning, we heard that Dewey and Warren had been nominated. "Thank God for America and it's way of life," we said, and started out for Glendo on the Trail, singing in the rain, happy in the thought that tomorrow would be Sunday and we could rest over the Sabbath Day.

That morning, stopping at the cafe run by Kay Vincent, we had a happy hour swapping stories with some cowboys who were eating breakfast in the place. At the close of the meal they looked carefully over our outfit and seemed pleased with it, especially the saddles. When we started to pay for our coffee, we were informed by the good mistress of the place that our money was no good, and, putting a wonderful sandwich lunch in our hands, told us we better get going.

We did, and had scarcely moved a block when we were stopped on the street by Dr. Wise, who said, "You are riding early; I'll bet you have had no breakfast. Come, let us have breakfast together." Do you wonder that we say it was good to come to Douglas, Joe Louis fight or no Joe Louis fight?

As we rode along this day the nature of the country seemed to change greatly; there was a ranker growth of vegetation, the air seemed to be heavier and more humid; the country seemed more like the Iowa and Nebraska which we had known as children. We passed the spot where Jim Bridger had once operated a ferry. Along this stretch we found the flies very annoying. The Pack twisted and kicked and turned over, smashing up things in general.

We were happy to get to Glendo, and to camp on another of the gem-like parks of the Conoco Oil Company. Many a time since, two weary travelers have thanked this great company for their hospitality to utter strangers. We could see from our camp, the scars of the Old Trail leading away northwest over the hills.

Glendo will remain in our memory as one of the brightest spots along the trail. Dear were the little children, everyone in town, who came over to visit the camp. Delightful was the service we held in the Episcopal Church. The man who took up the offering, we were informed later, kept a bar and was the leading gambler in the community. I doubted this story. At any rate, it was with real dignity, and I am persuaded with real piety, that he officiated that day.

We had intended to sleep in a little while this Sunday morning, but, about five o'clock, we heard a commotion among the baggage. The Pack had broken loose, drunk up the water in the collapsible pail, nosed around and turned over the pile of saddles, kicked over the sack of oats, and was helping herself to everything before her. We were provoked, though it was the Sabbath Day, and threatened to send her back to Portland. Her only answer was a whinny of delight so we changed our minds. The spilled and wasted oats were replaced by Bill Trenholm, who was of the opinion that traveling horses should not have to fast even on Sunday.

Monday morning we breakfasted with James Gamble, the

son of a Presbyterian minister, who served us coffee from a singing coffee pot. We felt it would be well if every meal could be enlivened with such music and song. The horses were sprayed with D.D.T., a futile effort to outsmart the terrible plague of flies, and we moved out across the prairie on the Old Trail. It was hard to say good-by to the citizens of this friendly little community, and especially to the family of Peter Miller, who were all out to say good-by and good luck.

We passed by Horseshoe Creek, where there had been a station of the pony express and stage coach. Who could pass by this part of the Trail without being deeply moved by it's story. Horseshoe Creek had been a favorite camping ground, with plenty of wood, water and grass. It was a logical situation for the stage station which was located here. The attack upon this isolated station, and its heroic defense by a handful of men, is one of the most thrilling stories of the West. An old settler informed us that Chief Crazy Horse led his seventy Ogallala Sioux against the place on a March morning in 1868, burning it to the ground. The three brave men defended the place until its walls were burnt down about them, then tunnelled out from beneath the burning ruins, and escaped. As we rode by we could almost hear the war cry and see the walls going down in flames.

We took off across a flat some miles in extent, then climbed a hill. At its top, we found an Old Oregon Trail marker standing by the trail which had been forever abandoned.

We descended a dry creek bed, crossed another, and camped on Big Cottonwood Creek, where the Old Trail had crossed. In this vicinity we had quite a battle with a big rattler. We had only a short riding crop and did not dare to get too close. I would strike at his head and he would draw back and strike at my hand. After several missing blows, I turned the crop around and swung the loaded butt down upon the snake's coils, thus putting him out. Obeying the Scriptural admonition, "The heel of the woman shall bruise the head of the serpent," I ground his vicious diamond-shaped skull into the earth with the heel of a riding boot. He was about three feet long. He had eight rattles and a button.

That night when doing our usual camp chores, we jumped at any movement in the grass. We made sure that the tent was securely closed against the entrance of even an insect, but slept poorly. We had already been told that the snakes were decidedly numerous in this particular region this year.

Our camp this night was in a beautiful cottonwood grove on the banks of the creek. Some of these trees must have seen the campfires of many a traveler, and the white-winged wagons may have drawn up in a great circle around the very spot on which our tent stood. One could almost hear in the winds among the branches the crackle of the campfires, the shout and laughter of those long-ago travelers.

These musings finally drove away the fear of the serpents and we rested well for the remainder of the night in our "Camp of the Rattlers" at the Old Cottonwood Crossing.

XI

EAGLE'S NEST

We were told we would find the Eagle's Nest not far beyond Guernsey, on the south side of the Platte, near Register Cliff. We expected to camp near this spot on our next day's ride. We got on the way as soon as possible, riding on or very near the Old Trail. The camp down by the Cottonwood Crossing soon became just a dream of interest, largely because of the rattler. We passed the Cold Springs Camping Ground, with the rifle pits on the brow of the hill, five hundred feet or so on our left. They were marked as of 1841.

While we were eating lunch at Guernsey, the old Pack walked off with the porch posts to which she had been tied. The proprietor of the cafe said there was no expense for the damage and good-naturedly nailed the post back in place. Here we met Paul Henderson, an authority on the Old Trail, at whose home at Bridgeport we were later entertained. That night we camped in a pasture belonging to Roy Cundall. It was made a fine evening by the visit of several people to our camp, and especially with two little fellows who built a fireplace and brought wood and water for the evening fire and meal. After dinner the people of the town gathered at the church, where they had a reception for us and heard the story of our journey.

Across the river from our camp, we could see the white stone marking the grave of a pioneer woman who had died on the way. The long, long trail had exacted a heavy price of those who followed it. By now we well knew how hard was the labor of just riding, riding, riding. It was natural that the aged, the frail, and the sickly would grow weary and lay them down in their final rest.

Just outside of Guernsey, we crossed to the south side of the Platte and rode through a meadowland of white flowers that looked like poppies, then through clouds of cheerful sunflowers. It is said that the Mormons on their trek to the West scattered sunflower seeds along the way. The Mormon Trail went along the north shore of the Platte and these plants were along the south shore; but sunflowers, as well as most other growing things could travel far in one hundred years.

The Platte River here was a wide band of silver running through an open park, with great cottonwood trees every--where. Riding along in the freshness of the morning, we were so entranced with the bright landscape that we had forgotten the Eagles's Nest for which we had been looking, till I heard a sudden call from Mrs. Beard, "Oh, look, there they are." And, sure enough, there they were, high up on the gray cliffs along which we had been riding. Some hundred or more feet down from the crest were the two nests of the eagles. They looked to be about six or eight feet in diameter, made of long entangled branches, surely a fit landmark for anyone riding the trail. We halted for some minutes and looked for a path that we might climb up to view these nests more carefully, but they were inaccessible to anything save good, strong wings.

Near the nests we passed the marker of the Old Pony Express, 1861-62. A little farther on we came to Register Cliff, where hundreds of names cut in the rock told the story of man's longing for the immortality of his name. Time with his great eraser had smoothed many of them from sight, and in another century will have his great cliff slate wiped clean.

Close to the face of the rock are several graves of the early travelers, also the grave of an Indian. This Register Cliff, though set aside by the government as a monument of the past, is within the rather spacious ranch of the Fredericks family, who have many relics of the Indian days, including a pair of two-wheeled carts pulled by the Mormons on their trek to Salt Lake.

The Old Trail ran through the gates of this ranch and down across the flats to the junction of the river and the cliffs four or five miles to the southeast. There it takes up over Mexican Hill. We followed it across the meadowland, climbing from the Platte bottom, on the very tracks where it ascended the steep hill. We got into some terribly rough country and it seemed for a time as if we must turn back. Soon, however, we found a wire running north and south and figured that any place where men have gone to string wire, they would have had horses to pull up the single strands and we believed that anywhere another man could go with his horse, we could.

Our horses, being range animals, were used to rough country. I rode ahead on Old Dynamite. The Pack, turned loose, would follow in his very steps, and Mrs. Beard on Black Fairy brought up the rear, urging Diamond on if she faltered. Sometimes the horses would almost fall over backwards as they climbed, and again they would simply slide down on their haunches. The sweat poured off our foreheads and we would pause at intervals to get our breath. At some points it seemed that we would not be able to continue. At the worst place in the climb, we paused almost too long, for the longer one hesitates in a difficult situation, the less likely is he to go on. Looking back, I saw Mrs. Beard with her lips closely compressed and not a sign of turning back.

Then, do you know, I seemed to see that blamed little old weazened-up shrimp of a cowpoke, and to hear him say, "I know I can ride it, but I don't think you can."

"Oh, is that so," I said to myself. I put the spurs into Old Dynamite's flank, he leaped the ugly looking gulch, the Pack cleared it far beyond necessary margin and Black Fairy skimmed over it as if on wings.

We climbed on up to the crest of the hill where we found a shallow road scraped off by the blade of a tractor or cat. We followed it east and, after several hours of fast and steady riding, came to a point where we could look down upon Old Fort Laramie. Here we paused for some time, resting in the saddles.

"Well, there it is," I said to Mrs. Beard.

"Just think, Lou, here is old Fort Laramie, a place we have so long wanted to see, one of the most historic spots in America. It was the first real outfitting and supply post on the Old Trail. It seemed a long ways off from Portland, where we first began our ride, didn't it? It seemed a long ways off when we were at Fort Dalles, at Fort Hall, at Fort Bridger, and even at Fort Caspar, but here it is at last. Fort Laramie! It pays just t keep going, doesn't it? It pays to travel, travel, travel. Marcus Whitman was right. Well, let's get going."

And we came down over the hill to Old Fort Laramie, near where Laramie Creek or river flows into the Platte. The old trapper or Mountain Man who selected sites for their trading posts, supply stations or forts certainly knew their stuff. This place, to use a clumsy but descriptive phrase, was certainly get-at-able for the wagon trains that would later plow their way up the plains of the Platte, and it was suitable for defense.

When the government needed such a fort from which to guard and patrol the country, they wisely bought this trading post. That was in 1849 and so Old Fort William became Fort John, then later Fort Laramie, and down through the stirring days of the century it remained Fort Laramie.

So long as the history of America is recited, so long as the tale of the Old Oregon Trail is told, it will continue to be romantic, fascinating Old Fort Laramie.

Down on the flat lands near the banks of the Laramie, perhaps a hundred yards from the nearest building of the Fort, is a timbered park. Here the grass grew tall and green. Here we pitched our camp and prepared to stay for several days, but, the best laid plans of mice and men, even about staying in camping spots, sometimes go awry and ours did here.

We had not reckoned on such a small thing as a gnat wrecking our plans, but that is exactly what happened. Just about sunset these insects began to make their presence known. They came in swarms so that the ungloved hand, used to brush them from the face, seemed to be meeting some elastic substance, which closed about it like thin, soft dough. When brushed down the breasts of the horses, my hand dripped blood. Next morning, the horses looked worn and drawn. As soon as we could get saddled up we were on our way. Though we had been able to remain but one evening and night, we visited all the old buildings still standing and recalled to memory much of the history of this romantic old fort.

It was six hundred and sixty-seven miles from Independence. It was the first supply station built on the Old Oregon Trail. Its history probably started when a French trapper, De la Ramee, set up a small trading post near where the later fort stood. This trapper had either been drowned in the river which bears his name, or had been killed by the Indians. Two men who had been with Ashley in 1822, Robert Campbell and William Sublette, probably built the first real stockade sometime in June, 1834. It was sold to Milton Sublette and Jim Bridger in 1835. They spent ten thousand dollars in its rehabilitation. Its old walls, made of sun-dried brick, had witnessed many stirring events and hilarious carousals. Many great names figured in the stories told of this old fort, such as Kit Carson, Jim Bridger, Jim Baker, Jim Beckwourth.

At Fort Bridger, we heard the story of a famous drunken shooting-match between Jim Bridger and Bill Jackson, in which, to prove their mutual friendship and trust, each man shot from the head of the other a tin cup filled with whiskey. This event was supposed to have taken place at Fort Bridger. When we arrived at Fort Laramie, we heard the same story, told with some minor variations, as taking place there. This rather colorful as well as whiskeyful story was recited as authentic history, though we, of course, took it *cum grano salis*. It probably does have some elements of historic truth. Something like it must have happened in the early days, for in the great novel, *The*

Covered Wagon, by Emerson Hough, such a shooting match is told with breath-taking power. Too, John G. Neihardt, in *The Song of Three Friends* centers his whole poem, with most dramatic effect, about such a shooting and the death of one of the principals. Our question concerning the truth or fiction of this story is about the whiskey in the tin cups. Had the cups been filled with water, or had they been just plain empty cups of tin, we might believe the tale, but it is utterly beyond belief that either Jim Bridger or Bill Jackson, Mike Fink, or Carpenter, would have risked the precious whiskey in such a reckless way.

At one time or another, Francis Parkman, Sheridan, Miles Kearney, all glorified this place with their presence. On June 21, 1836, Mrs. Spalding and Narcissa Whitman found brief recuperation and enjoyed the luxury of comfortable, skin-bottomed chairs amidst this wild setting. Here also history records that Whitman left one of his cherished wagons.

Most of our night here, we spent in recalling and discussing the romantic stories of the old post. It was with real sorrow we saddled up and left, but we could not subject our horses to further agony from the insect pests.

Thunder storms, thirst, hunger, flies, and mosquitoes, all these things made the life of the early emigrant miserable at times. We experienced all of these trials except hunger. We were very thankful that we, too, could take it.

Riding out through the little town of Fort Laramie, a mile or two north of the fort, we were happy to meet the minister, the Reverend George Woodard. We found him the same quiet, gentle, grace-filled man we had known in the seminary.

Before we came into the town, we crossed over to the Old Mormon Trail north of the river on perhaps the oldest bridge west of the Missouri River. Its iron beams had been hauled the whole way from the Missouri River by ox team.

The ride this day was very hot, hard, and trying. Somewhere along this stretch of the Platte, probably on the south side, may be the grave of young Lieutenant Gratton, killed August 17, 1874. No one whom we contacted seemed to know where the exact spot is . The twenty-eight companions who fell with him are buried at Fort McPherson. His body may lie at Ft. Leavenworth. Just lately we have learned that it does

We were caught in a heavy downpour of rain just as we entered Torrington, but we paused until it was over, taking shelter under some magnificent old cottonwood trees. What with our chaps and hooded marine slickers, we were dry and comfortable through the ride. And in our little tent, pitched in the fair grounds, we were dry and well sheltered from the rain that fell all that night.

We rode hard all the next day, with little excitement except a battle between Dynamite and the Pack, who had started action just as I was mounting Dynamite after a roadside lunch. They smashed me against a big cottonwood tree, almost catching my leg between the saddle and the trunk of the tree. However, I lifted my leg in time and the rifle (the very pride of my heart, a 32 Special Winchester Carbine) in its boot under the stirrup leather caught the force of the impact. The stock was broken squarely off. But one can't cry long over spilt milk, nor moan over a wrecked gun, so with, "Well, I should worry," we began singing our marching song, "A Roaming in the Gloaming," and took off down the trail to Mitchell.

Outside the town, we were met by the newspaper man, Mr. Snyder, who had arranged for us to camp at the fair grounds. The Clint Morrisons from Scottsbluff came out to visit us here and made arrangements for us to go to their ranch, which is right on the Old Trail going through Mitchell Pass. Tom Green of the Oregon Trail Association, came out to the camp also and ate dinner with us. We made camp, cooked dinner and washed the dishes in the dark that night.

Next morning we rode into Scottsbluff. Outside the city we were met by the Riding Club, some twenty-five gaily-clothed riders on sleek, spirited horses. After a parade through the city, our horses were put in the pasture of Owen Frank. There was a fine dinner and reception that night at the hotel. Again we told the story of our ride thus far along the trail. History certainly lives in Scottsbluff and centers around the two passes, the Robidoux and the Mitchell, by which the wagons passed through the great hill called Scott's Bluff.

We spent Saturday, July third visiting as many of the things of historic interest as time permitted. With Mr. Tom Green, Harry Wisner, and Winfield Evans, all sons of pioneers, we visited the grave of Rebecca Winters. Here a great railway ran, and had been turned aside lest it should disturb her sleep. A wagon tire with the date of her death had been placed above this pioneer woman's grave. The wagon tire is still there with its legend, chisled at night by A. M. Reynolds, but now a granite marker also tells the story and on it are the words:

IN MEMORY OF REBECCA BURDICK,
WIFE OF HIRAM WINTERS.
She died a faithful Latter Day Saint.
August 15, 1852.

While making that memorable journey across the plains with her people to find a new home in the far distant Salt Lake Valley, she gave her life for her faith.

This monument was erected in 1902, her centennial year, by her numerous descendants in Utah. It is said that at her grave the Mormon people gather every year and sing their song of hope:

And should we die before our journey's through
Happy day, all is well.

We also stood at the resting place of another. On the stone the words:

Daughter of a soldier of the Revolution,
Our beloved mother, she was carried all day
to this spot and buried.

Of this one, the story goes that the party had been troubled and harassed all day by a band of Indians begging for food and pilfering and could not be sent away. Finally they uncovered the face of the dead; her face scarred with marks of smallpox that had taken her life, struck such terror into the hearts of the Indians that they departed in panic haste.

Up in the Robidoux Pass, following a dim trail, we came to another group of Pioneer graves. On a stone above them, we read this inscription:

Honoring these and all the thousands,
Who lie in nameless graves along the Trail.
Faith and courage such as theirs made America.
May ours preserve it.

At Scottsbluff, in the life of Harry Wisner, we find all the hopes, pain and success of pioneer people and their children, in fact, a picture of much of the life along the Old Trail. The grandfather of Mr. Wisner had come across the plains in 1850-51. He was never heard from after he crossed the Missouri River. He left behind a wife, three boys, and a little girl. The next year, the wife and mother (another Evangeline) went on the quest to find the loved husband. She too, disappeared after she had crossed the Missouri. And here was a grandchild who had followed the trek into the setting sun to the vicinity of Scottsbluff. Here he had settled, and, an old man today, he is honored and respected as one of the finest and most successful of his generation. Of such stuff was the pioneer, of such stuff are the children.

Through the courtesy of Mr. Green, we were taken up through the Robidoux Pass to the vicinity of Signal Rock. Now, not only the hundred years of Old Trail history came back as we gazed on this rock, but hundreds of centuries of unwritten history unfolded before us. There the excavations and exploration have revealed strata of dust formed out of successful occupations. Here through the fleeting centuries, tribe and race succeeded tribe and race; they lived; kindled their campfires; posted their sentries; sent forth their signals; then had moved on across the eternal ranges.

At almost the crest of this pass, Robidoux had once had a small supply station, a trading post, and a blacksmith shop. The charge for horseshoeing was about what I had to pay—a dollar and a quarter a shoe. When someone else used the tools and did the work, he was charged seventy-five cents an hour and twenty-five cents apiece for the horseshoe nails. It is on record that a government explorer, visiting this place in 1849-50, had his mules shod here and did the work himself.

Just over the brow of the hill from where the shop stood, we found three great green rings where the grass was of a much deeper color, as if a three-ringed circus had once **stood** there. The outward rims of the grass were about fifteen feet wide and the diameter of each ring seventy-five or a hundred feet. These rings probably marked where wagon train after wagon train, through the years, had drawn up in circles for the night's camp and protection from sudden attack. The post and the blacksmith shop were later destroyed by the Indians.

Not far along, we drank from the Robidoux Springs. We followed up a little trickle of water, running through the deep gulch, to where, amid a thicket of rose bushes and brush, it gurgled out of a rock. This perhaps was the very spring from which Francis Parkman drank and which he describes in his *Oregon Trail.* It is possible that Father De Smet drank from this spring and with its clear, pure water baptized the little half-Indian children of Robidoux.

Later in the day, we climbed with our guides to the top of Scottsbluff itself and looked, as far as the eye could reach, over a vast irrigated garden. We felt as Abraham must have felt when he lifted up his eyes and saw the Valley of the Jordan, well watered everywhere like the garden of the Lord, as thou comest into Zoar.

But we looked west also, up the valley of the Platte, and recalled that the fair, homey city below and this bluff took their names from the wounded, deserted man who had crawled from near Fort Laramie — some sixty miles — to die here by the spring that gurgled from somewhere near its base.

Words can never tell the deep satisfaction that was ours as we surveyed these chapters of the past as written in the records of this stern, old bluff. We longed to stay and visit every part of the ground, but we were pilgrims of the sunrise and had to ride along into the morning. So early on July 5 we were on our way .

XII

WINDLASS HILL

IF ONE IS GOING TO GO FAR, WHETHer on foot or horseback, he needs always to keep the final destination in view but he also should have fixed intermediate points to be reached within certain time limits. Every stage of our journey had been made easier and more interesting because of limited objectives. We did not ride the whole Trail at once but did ride continuously with our entire attention fixed on each new goal. When we left Scottsbluff our marks were Windlass Hill and Ash Hollow and along that way we would be watching, as did the old pioneer but in reverse order, for Chimney Rock and Court House Rock.

On Monday, July 5, we rode through Gering without stopping. We had planned to spend some time here but we were beginning to feel the urge to be on our way. The journey began to seem long, and we found hard going. The flies, the mosquitoes, and the heat all tried our patience and sapped much of our strength as we rode.

That night, we camped near Chimney Rock and remarked, as we kept it in sight through the day, how like the Statue of Liberty it looked there above the sea of cornfields and cultivated terrain. It had indeed been a Statue of Liberty to the early travelers, the liberty and the freedom of the untamed West.

Our camp was not three hundred yards from where the Old Trail ran and where its marks could still be seen. Here we had a pretty rough time of it with another infestation of mosquitoes. We stayed awake all night long, keeping a smudge fire going, making thick clouds of smoke in which the horses could stand to fend off their tormentors. The only relief we had was to crawl into our mosquito-proof tent between fires. It was a dreaded ordeal to crawl out of the protection of the canvas to replenish the smoking pile with green grass and weeds.

Through Bridgeport and Broadwater we rode, always in

sight of Court House Rock. The rock is well named, it looks like some old Greek temple, whose builders had long since passed beyond the reach of all laws made by man.

From now on, most of our journey lay between wire fences and cultivated fields. On this day's ride, we found the Old and the New side by side, yet markedly contrasted. On one side of the road, a mother and father and several children were cutting, binding, and shocking their harvest of wheat. On the other side, in a field that extended far beyond over the hills in three directions, several combines were cutting, reaping, threshing the wheat and scattering the chaff over the field, all in one continuous operation.

One method had something of sentiment in it. Seeing the family, we instinctively thought of Ruth and Boaz and their ancient field of golden corn. The other scene had modern efficiency, but we thought of assembly lines, machines, nervous speed, and spiritual exhaustion.

That day on the highway, where it was impracticable to travel along on the shoulders and where the view of the road was unobstructed for miles, we barely escaped being run down by a speeding machine, which almost ditched itself on the wrong side of the road. When the man at the wheel ground his car to a stop, then stepped on the gas to get away without saying a word, we laughed and said, "Well, the pioneer had wild Indians but we have drunken drivers."

As we crossed over the bridge to Broadwater, thousands of swallows came gracefully from beneath it, as if to welcome us to the little city.

From Broadwater to Oshkosh was a day's ride. Here Earl Wright, a man much interested in the Old Trail and a great community worker as well, arranged for a meeting of the Chamber of Commerce, then for a city get-together. We delivered here the greetings of the Oregon Trail Association. We visited an old historic spring south of town, and many other places and things of interest. That night, declining the hearty invitation of Mr. Wright to spend the night in his home, we slept in the pasture with our horses, who seemed so glad for our presence that they kept us awake most of the night. The air mattresses were as soft as down and we really rested. Man needs but little after all.

We were escorted out of Oshkosh by Joe Anne Casey on her beautiful, black, blooded horse. She made a very fetching picture with the silver-mounted black saddle and her graceful carriage.

We arrived at storied Ash Hollow at about three o'clock. Our camp was made at the ranch of Roy Wolff. A freshet, pouring with unaccustomed fury over a part of his ranch, had caused considerable damage the week before but he was not in the least downcast. He asked us to remain at his place over the Sabbath Day. He promised that he would conduct us to spots of historic interest—the old cemetery, the place of the trading post down near the river, the cave up on the bluff across the trail, and finally to Windlass Hill.

Up in the old cave, after much digging, we found a large, rusty knife that had evidently been beaten out by hand. The cave probably had once been occupied by Indians and later, so we were told, by a band of outlaws.

At Ash Hollow we visited the grave of Rachel Patterson who died in 1849. She belonged to a California emigrant train coming out of Missouri. She was only eighteen years of age. We noted how the Trail took heavy toll of youth.

Just a short way from the cemetery had been the box, a sort of wayside post office, where the early travelers would deposit their letters and from which the letters would find their way east or west.

About a half mile west of Ash Hollow, we found the cliff over which the Indians were accustomed to stampede and kill the buffalos on their hunting expeditions. This seemed to have been a rather common but successful method of securing the desired meat.

Nine miles northeast of Ash Hollow on Blue Creek is the place of the actual battle, often called the Battle of Ash Hollow, where Brigadier-General William S. Harney's men fought with the Brule Sioux in 1855, killing eighty Indians and losing twelve soldiers. Lieutenant Gratton's massacre had finally been avenged.

It was not far away, on this same Blue Creek, that Red Cloud, the Indian Chief, was born. Here at Ash Hollow, on August 7, 1837, W. H. Gray, of the Presbyterian Mission at Lapwai, barely escaped with his life. Four of his Indian escort were killed.

Late on this Sunday afternoon, we crawled through a barbed wire fence, took our way across a pasture, and climbed for some little distance up a rapidly steepening hill. Soon we paused to catch our breath; looking up, we saw several rather shallow gullies coming down from the crest of the hill, running along side by side.

Windlass Hill! We had not only seen it, we had stood on its summit. That moment was worth all the cost, the labor, the hardships of our ride. Here at the top of the hill stood a lonesome, single stone. It was a marker on the Old Trail. It stood in the place where the windlass or huge post had been fixed by means of which the great, white-covered conestoga wagons had been let down the grade. The descending wagons had made ruts; these washed by the storms of a hundred years, made the gullies we saw.

From the hill-top marker, we could follow the Old Trail as far as we could see in the gathering dusk. We could hardly sleep when we turned in. We were living in the Yesterday of a hundred years ago. That night, from far across Windlass Hill down to our tent in Ash Hollow, came the lonesome cry of a coyote. It was a cry out of that Yesterday which shall never be again, forever.

Monday night we spent in Ogallala, where the cattle trails of by-gone days came up from the south. A boisterous dust storm, which turned into a severe electric storm, beat down upon our tent, but we were soon lulled to sleep by the night-long fall of gentle rain which succeeded the thunder and lightning.

We reached Paxton after a hard, trying ride and put up the tent under a cottonwood tree. When we unsaddled the horses, we were sickened by the sight of a great saddle sore that had developed on the withers of Black Fairy. She had been such a quick, active, friendly little thing, and had responded so readily to every wish of her mistress that it did not seem right for her to suffer the pain of this terrible sore. When it was treated and dressed with white gauze secured with adhesive tape, she looked like a soldier who had won his decoration in battle. We thought her to be just that, a good soldier, but now grieviously wounded. We decided to give her a furlough for a few days.

On the ride in, I suddenly became aware that the Old Pack was not doing the usual rearing back or plunging from side to side on the trail. Looking around, I found that I had carelessly dropped the lead rope and she was almost a quarter of a mile away, heading back toward Portland. Every time the chance offered she would start back. I think, by all the odds, she was the most perverse critter I have ever seen.

That day we saw myriads of blue and purple morninglories and golden mountains of grain, threshed and waiting to be sent to the elevator and to the mills.

That night, it stormed. I have never heard such vicious and continuous thunder in my life. All night long it continued and again, we found ourselves longing for a thunder-proof tent and one thick enough to keep out the glare of the lightning.

Well, neither night nor a thunder storm can last forever, and morning came at last. And what a sight met our eyes. All three horses were plastered with mud from hoof to ears. We finally got them fairly well curried and saddled but decided Black Fairy's sore was too severe for the saddle. So Mrs. Beard took the stage to North Platte. I took the three horses, minus one saddle on by trail.

What a day I had. The distance was thirty-two miles, every mile a fight, first with Old Dynamite, who did not want to be bothered with two self-willed fillies that were forever trying to get ahead of him, then with big, black horse-flies, little black nose flies, then mosquitoes. But all's well that ends well. About five miles out of North Platte, three riders came to meet me. Two of them took the extra horses in tow and the other rode alongside.

It was a great relief just to drop the two lead ropes. My arms were aching as though they would fall from their sockets. At the palatial stable of J. B. Bowman, the horses were put in box-stalls away from the flies and mosquitoes. The tent was pitched on the green grass in the yard and the campfire was lighted.

The good bacon and hot coffee, the watermelon furnished by our host, the joy of being reunited with my family, made me soon forget the hard day's labor. That evening many a tall tale of adventure was told by ourselves, our host, and friends alike. As the big hours gave way to the small hours of the night, we said it was good to be riding the Old Oregon Trail and to be meeting with new friends all along the way.

We were now in North Platte, Bill Cody's old home. His ranch house is just outside the limits of the city. The big old barn, with letters which Cody himself had painted on it, shows how young we yet are, and how near our Today is to our Yesterday.

Just yesterday, Buffalo Bill was hunting buffalo where the city stands and in the country where the great transcontinental railway goes. It seems but yesterday when I myself saw Buffalo Bill in all the full regalia of his Wild West Show. What a handsome fellow he was and what a wonderful shot.

We spent four days here in North Platte. We met several of the citizens of this stirring place. We visited the extensive experimental farm where the elk and the buffalo are still kept. We visited the great irrigation project, and the Sioux look-out on the high hill south of town. We preached in the Presbyterian church. We had all three horses shod. A good veterinarian doctored the sore on Black Fairy. The sores on the Pack were practically healed. We broadcasted an interview over KODY and, after giving the city greetings from the Oregon Trail Association we prepared for the final five hundred miles of the ride over the Trail.

Just before we left, we received a long-distance call from Minden and an invitation from the Kearney Saddle and Bridle Club to be their guests.

XIII

THE CHRISTMAS CITY

On Monday morning, July 19, at eight o'clock, we left Mr. Bowman's barn where we had camped for four most pleasant days and started out for Minden, the Christmas City, as our next objective. The horses, newly shod all around with good heavy shoes by an old cow hand who was an expert horseshoer, stepped out as if proud of their new irons and the ringing of their feet on the pavement. Mr. Bowman and Mrs. McNulty, on their splendid Palominos, escorted us four or five miles. Then we were picked up by an escort of police, who got us safely over a very long and quite dangerous bridge.

It was a beautiful morning, with a breeze blowing that cleared the air of mosquitoes and flies. The corn fields were green and heavy with filling ears; wild flowers were blooming and sending up sweet fragrance from every foot of the way; and the air was full of bird song.

The horses, refreshed by their long rest, wanted to burn up the miles. We made the twenty-four miles to Brady by four o'clock.

We camped at night on Brady Island, located in the Platte, twenty-five or thirty miles in length, and named after a Mr. Brady who had been killed by the Indians. Our camp was made in a pasture close to the spot where this tragedy had occured. It was an ideal campsite, as there was plenty of grass and water and wood for fire. Just over our heads, with it's delicious fruit now ripe, and with the branches heavily laden, a mulberry tree furnished us with dessert for supper and fresh fruit for breakfast. Ripe, black mulberries and sugar with condensed cream make a dainty dish for any meal.

Many people came out from Brady to visit around the campfire, among them the local newspaper editor and Mr. and Mrs. Ingrahm who had arranged for the camping place and who brought us oats for the horses. The night at this camp was excessively hot. We slept behind the mosquito netting but not under covers.

The next day we rode through a dreamland of many-colored flowers, blue, yellow, gorgeous purple. The Scotch thistle frequently waved to us, their pink banners turning to red, and the delicate blue morninglories, so frail and pure, came to our hearts as a prayer. The rain fell like soft mist all day long, making the ride a delight. It is fun to ride and sing in the rain.

Leaving the horses running loose in the rodeo grounds, after a chicken dinner, we went with the V. A. Underwoods for a long drive south of the river to find the Oregon Trail markers. Then we came back to our camp at Cozad, where the Riding Club of that town came out to visit us. Here we spent another happy evening around the campfire, hearing and telling tales of the early days.

We were told a story of the town of Lexington through which we were expecting to pass about noon on the following day.

It seems that Plum Creek, in the early days was a wide-open town, often visited by cowboys from the range, travelers along the Trail, and outlaws from many directions. Many men had fought and drank here, some had died, others had been hung, one man having been hung from the courthouse window.

When the railroad was built through Plum Creek, it's reputation for being a wild and wooly place was greatly increased and was widely and permanently established. A drunken cowboy was on the train one night. When he did not get off at the station, the conductor roused him to inquire as to his destination. The cowboy informed the conductor that he "was going to Hell" and wished the trainman to go to the same hot place. "Oh," replied the conductor, "we have just passed that place." Then he stopped the train, reversed the engine, backed up and put the cowboy off at Plum Creek. Soon after that the name of the town was changed to Lexington. Guess it was time.

Well, we found it a mighty fine little city amidst the fertile corn fields of Nebraska, a city whose roots are deeply grounded in the history of the West and the Old Oregon and Mormon

Trails. One chapter of that history has been dramatically told by Michael Delahunty in *Plumcreekers' History of the Trail Country.*

On the night of August 7, 1867, between Plum Creek and the present site of Darr occurred the railroad wreck, the story of which was published around the world. Shortly after dark, the Indians raised the rails and took down the telegraph wire. It has always been supposed that renegade whites helped the Indians, as they were afraid of the telegraph wires and someone was involved who knew how to manage raising the rails. The telegraph agent ordered the section men from Plum Creek to fix the telegraph wires and sent out Jim Delahunty and six other men. Indians appeared and attacked the men, who returned the fire. Pat Handerhand, was killed; a Mr. Thompson was scalped (he continued to live for several years and his scalp was on exhibit in Omaha); Pat Griswold was hit in the hip; the rest escaped uninjured. A freight train of about twenty-five cars ran into the trap and the Indians turned to the wreck.

The engineer and fireman were instantly killed and the conductor ran to Plum Creek to report and stop other trains. The Indians plundered the cars, set them on fire, and had a big dance. So great was the danger that everyone but Pat Delahunty and the Daniel family, who stayed to guard their property, boarded a train sent from farther east, and went on to Elm Creek where they spent the night in a sod doby. The next morning the party returned to the scene of the wreck. At Plum Creek, a flat car was hooked in front of the engine and, with guns and ammunition, they started toward the wreck. One of the boys in the party was Melvin Freeman, now living in Lexington. The engine stopped a mile from the smoking wreck, as the Indians were numerous. They were having a good time. One end of a bolt of calico was tied to each horse's tail, and they would ride dragging the rest behind. They also found two barrels of whisky. Pat Delahunty, a crack shot, picked the Indian who seemed to be the leader, and shot him. This caused the rest to scatter and run south toward the Malalley ranch. A troup of scouts came from Fort McPherson but the Indians had disappeared so they set to work to clean up the wreck.

Major North brought the Pawnee scouts. Upon word from the telegraph operator at old Fort Plum Creek south of the river, the scouts were sent to investigate, but found nothing. Three days later, another report came and this time, after a battle with the Indians, the scouts returned with sixteen scalps, thirty-five mules, saddles, a squaw and an Indian boy.

The scalps were placed on sticks and stuck in the ground along the track for the benefit of passengers on the trains. It was the idea of the scouts that the passengers would feel safer, but many were terrified by the idea that this was meant as a warning to them. The headquarters of the Pawnee scouts in Plum Creek was called Fort Hell.

We left Overton for Kearney early next morning, taking with us the gift of a dozen ears of sweet corn and a quart of luscious strawberries.

Just outside of Kearney, we were met by Everett Roberts of Corral Inn, Milton Kline and Mr. Fowles of the Kearney Riding Club, and a large number of riders, who escorted us to Corral Inn where the horses were put up for the night in sumptuous box stalls. The next morning the Old Pack leaped over the lower half of the door, smashing it from its hinges and skinning her hind legs in several places—because she wanted to fight another horse running loose in the yard. That evening, after a broadcast over the local station, we were entertained at a picnic dinner in Kearney's spacious Harmon Park. It takes a group of horse-lovers to have a time at a picnic dinner; this group were also lovers of historic things and well informed in the history and events of the Old Oregon Trail.

At Old Fort Kearney, about a half mile south of the Platte, we addressed a large gathering of pioneers and history-lovers of the state. There we heard some of the fascinating history which we later read in a very fine pamphlet, *A Brief History of Fort Kearney*, written by Dr. Lyle E. Mantor of the Nebraska State Teacher's College at Kearney, Nebraska:

"Nearly 50,000 emigrants passed over the Oregon Trail during the gold rush in 1849. There was little Indian danger until Fort Kearney was reached, but westward Indians were apt to be encountered at any time. Most of the gold seekers were inexperienced travelers and found it necessary to reorganize their trains at the fort. Often, from wagons too heavily laden, they discarded every possible item of equipment, and sometimes even food, to lighten loads for the long journey ahead. The stop to rest the animals, to repair outfits, and to reorganize trains, made the fort a very busy place during the travel season.

"Emigration began in the forties, continued through the fifties. A major portion of the overland travel to California and Oregon passed over the Oregon Trail. Fort Kearney became a fixed and established point on that trail, it's garrison affording protection in time of Indian danger and its storehouses providing food and supplies to stranded or impecunious travelers far from home. The commanding officer at the fort was authorized by a law to issue or sell supplies from the government warehouse, upon requisition, to such persons as he deemed worthy of aid. The officers were very careful about approving such requests, but despite this, many applications were accepted. Large numbers of persons were inexperienced in plains travel, and because of unwise selections of goods, found themselves in need when Fort Kearney was reached. Accident or robbery deprived others of food. The fort rendered necessary aid in these cases and an important service to those in distress."

The Pony Express Route lay through the Fort Kearney reservation and by 1860 a telegraph line reached and remained here as its western terminus till August, 1861. When we hear and know that in one year, 1860, more than 20,000,000 pounds of freight, hauled in 4,000 wagons, pulled by 40,000 oxen, and handled by 4,500 men and as many as 500 of the great freight wagons daily passed along the trail, we begin to understand the importance of this old fort.

Fort Kearney long was known for its hospitality and was often called, The Prairie Haven, for travelers on the Oregon Trail, and we found it a haven indeed, though not a single building remains. Cool and inviting was the grassy sward neath the spreading arms of the great oaks. The welcome extended to us by it's friendly citizens was truly heartening.

Paul Warp, president of the Minden Chamber of Commerce, was master of ceremonies, and he read to us a letter of generous welcome from Governor Val Peterson of Nebraska. State Senator Fred A. Mueller of Kearney and the State Park Commission extended greetings, as also did William Meier of Minden, and Charles A. Chapell, president of the Fort Kearney Memorial Association.

We felt like drawing our pack train into a circle and camping here for a long time. Mrs. George Rafferty, who owns a farm once part of the Old Fort site, thought it would be a good idea; then we could find, as she had found, many relics of its early days.

Excavation by skilled men, under the direction of L. A. Emerson of Lincoln, Nebraska, has recovered many artifacts, as well as revealed the foundations of many buildings. The Fort, built in 1848, is to be restored in many of its features and will stand as a monument to the heroic life that circled about its walls.

Just before we left the city of Kearney for the Fort, a tourist wanted to put on a Western costume and have his picture taken on Black Fairy, but, as her back was still quite sore, we had to refuse. We offered to let him have his picture taken on Old Dynamite, but this he was not ready to risk. I think it would have made a fine picture, especially a fine moving picture.

When we left the city, we were escorted out of town and two or three miles beyond the bridge over the Platte by the Riding Club.

It seemed as if the riders had scarcely left us, when looking down the road, we saw another long line of riders coming out to meet us and show us into Minden, the Christmas City.

Our visit here was one of the most enjoyable along the whole way. Minden is not directly on the Old Trail; it is some three or four miles south; but the Old Trail runs right through the heart of every one of its citizens. Especially does it run through that of Paul A. Warp, son of Oscar Warp of the publishing house of Warp and Company, a splendid young fellow, a lieutenant in the last great war. He was with the Riders Club now, and what a welcome they had prepared for us!

As we rode into the city and around the public square with the court house at it's heart, the carillon of bells within the tower began to play "America the Beautiful." At it's close a voice went out over the air, "Welcome, Chaplain and Mrs. Beard, riders of the Old Oregon Trail, Ambassadors of Good Will from the Oregon Trail Association of Oregon. Welcome to the Christmas City." We felt welcome indeed.

This city has found some of the real secrets of life. It is more than a prosperous little city amidst the rich, agricultural section of the Middle West. It is a great family, a place where every man's good seems to be every man's concern. Though it knows the push and planning of success, it also knows the cultural value of entertainment, fellowship, rest, leisure, and community pleasure.

One thing that is most alluring is the fact that Minden takes time off every day for a cup of coffee and a social hour together. Another thing, Minden observes the Christmas time and carries the Christmas spirit through the year. At Christmas time the great court house in the public square is illuminated with thousands upon thousands of many-colored lights. And at Christmas time, people from miles around come back to Minden, as children to their old home.

The evening we were there, the very night was turned into day under the white lights that flashed from the tower and from every window and corner of the building, down over the green sward below. A big crowd had gathered in the square, the carillon of bells played glorious music, and many fine things were said about the Old Trail, the Old Pioneer, Old Fort Kearney, and the other old far-off things. Many heart-warming things which we loved to hear, were said to us, the latest riders of this historic way.

Yes, it was a red-letter day on our ride into the sunrise. That night, after the public meeting in the square, we were taken to the home of Mrs. Mary Canaday, where we attended a meeting of the historical society.

Next day, conducted by Mrs. Mary D. Anderson and Mrs. Jennie Light, Mrs. Canaday and daughter Golda, we visited a grave, some seven miles out of Lowell, Nebraska, now made famous from the story of romantic love that has grown up around it. We are informed by the marker that it is the grave of Mrs. Susan O. Hail of Lafayette County, Missouri, who died June 2, 1852, age 34 years, 5 months and 12 days. She was supposed to have died from drinking water poisoned by the Indians. But most think it was from some common ailment.

Of this death we heard how, when it came, a brief, religious service was held and the body was consigned to it's rest. The sweet, solemn ritual of the Church was intoned, "Earth to earth, ashes to ashes, dust to dust." Then the bull-whack sounded; the sad, tired oxen swung slowly into line; and the wagon train lost itself in the gathering dusk of the evening, moving on toward that faraway home beyond the plains and the hills. But the young husband did not go with the train. He knelt beside the new-made grave, lifted up his voice in prayer, then turned and took his lonesome, solitary way back across the plains to Independence, Missouri, where he secured a headstone which he placed in a wheelbarrow and, with his own unassisted strength, brought it back and placed it above the grave. Then, with a parting prayer of resignation but of hope he too, set his face toward the West.

We heard many versions of the story of the lone grave there on the plains of the Platte. Some question it's authenticity. As for us, we want to and do believe it is so. It is good for us in this modern day, when old-fashioned loves and ways are often scorned, to have this story of sweet and romantic love from that lonesome mound come to us as the scent of wild roses blowing across the prairie lands of life. May it thrill many a soul through the years to come. May it bring a tender glow to the heart of every one who, riding the Old Trail, will turn aside and pause to recall this old, old story.

Here at Christmas City I received one of the finest compliments of my ministerial career. Through the church services on Sunday morning, one of the worshippers seemed to be listening intently. He was a man of about my own age, with a fine, earnest face. He waited at the door for me. Putting out his hand, he grasped mine with a vice-like grip and, looking me full in the face and without a smile, said, "That was a hell of a good sermon." And I know he meant it. When I unclasped my aching fingers, I found he had left a matter of fifteen dollars in my hand. It made me happy to think that one man, at least, had thought my sermon worth that much. Through the years a great multitude had voted they were worth from five to twenty-five cents—about twenty cents the average.

I am laughing to myself now as I recall another curious happening on this ride on the trail. Over in Wyoming, coming to a cafe and tavern along the way, and being quite tired and thirsty, we had stopped to get a malted milk. Just as we finished and were getting ready to mount, some cowboys, perhaps a trifle too happy, came out of the tavern and over to our horses. They inspected their shoes, admired the hand-tooled saddles, asked if I could use the lariat suspended from the saddle tree. Then looking up and seeing the crosses I always wore on my collar, one remarked, "What, are you a preacher?"

On being informed I was, he explained, "Well, I'll be damned, a preacher riding through the country with chaps, spurs, and a rope. Can you use that rope? Can you hit anything with that gun?"

Then, reaching down in his Levis, he drew out a shining silver dollar and, taking off his hat, weather-beaten and much the worse for wear, threw the coin into it. Holding the reins of my horse in one hand and the hat in the other, he called to those standing around, "We're going to take up a collection. No damned preacher is going to ride through our country without a collection. Come on, now, throw in."

He had the real power of leadership, for when the last one had passed by and deposited his offering, the hat contained seventeen dollars and fifty cents. Gathering it up, with the green backs showing through his fingers and with a few small silver coins squeezing out and falling on the ground, he reached up and thrust the burden of coins into my shirt pocket. When I remonstrated, not too strenuously, of course, that we had plenty to take care of us clear through, without any collection or assistance, he muttered, "Well, that's all right, just keep what you got, this won't hurt you none. No damned preacher is going to ride through here without a collection."

And turning about, he rode away, and we rode down the trail.

That night we had moonlight on the desert—not moonshine but moonlight—and by it's light we looked back into the generous heart of a cowboy.

On an excursion this day at Minden we found some names of ranches which were redolent of the past. One had been called Dirty Woman's Ranch, another Lazy Man's Ranch, and still another Dirty Man's Ranch.

At Laurel, through which we rode, we saw the great cottonwood tree that had been planted by Judge Goglin in 1876 when Lowell was the county-seat.

On Monday morning we rode away from Minden with the strains of Aloha floating out from the carillon of bells from the court house tower. Some day we want to ride back again, and we hope the bells will be playing, "O Beautiful for Spacious Skies," the song that welcomed us the first time.

At Norman, a little lad and lass, Wesley Shannon and Helen Bergsten, came out on their ponies to take us to the home of Mr. and Mrs. Harry Bergsten for a wonderful chicken dinner. We did not tarry too long at this meal, for the weather had now begun to look threatening again and we wanted to keep pretty well to our schedule.

We passed through Holstein and came on down to Roseland. Here we had just camped, when Harry Perdum, the circulating manager of the Hastings *Tribune*, arrived with a car to take us over to Hastings for a dinner and a visit to it's House of Yesterday, one of the finest museums in America. In it the old days are truly made to live again. We found an old stage coach and a conestoga wagon so well preserved that one could harness them up and drive again into the West along the Old Trail. Especially noteworthy is the display of wild life pictured in native surroundings.

On the way over to Hastings that night we were overtaken by one of the heaviest rain storms we have ever passed through. The rain fell in such torrents that no car could drive through it. So we stopped right on the highway until the storm had passed. But we returned through a glorious night, with the white moon breaking through the clouds, to find our little tent on an elevated ridge under a thick hedge, all dry and cozy.

Next morning, through a world new washed and golden, we passed on our way toward the last log cabin on the Trail.

XIV

LONE CABIN ON THE TRAIL

On Tuesday Morning, July 27, we looked from our little tent upon a crimson sunrise. With a song we passed across the border of Kansas, the state which marked the last leg of the long journey.

Through the well-drenched corn fields we rode to Ayer. Here we sought water for the horses but found none until a cook in a cafe took a dishpan and carried a drink to them.

That night we camped at Spring Ranch in a lush meadow on the bank of the Blue, where we heard one of the gruesome stories that simply will not die with the years. It concerned a woman who had cut up her hired help and fed some two or three of them to the hogs. We found that the tale of the number murdered differed; some said one, some said two, some said three. We were shown the little bridge from which three of the murder gang had been hanged.

At Spring Ranch there had been a stage station on the Overland Route. Near here was the old Pawnee Ranch. We visited the grave of Francis Huff. The original stone, or rather what remains of it, has been encased in cement, and on it we found a rather remarkable inscription:

Francis Huff of Marshall County, Indiana
Died June 19, 1860

Remember friends as you pass by
As you are now, so once was I
As I am, so you must be.
Remember this, and think of me.

Well, that was a generation of preachers, if we can judge from what we find on their monuments. We have often remembered the sermon we read there.

We sobered down somewhat as we rode on through the swarms of flies, which seemed to be more vicious than usual. Then, too, we had a close call in an unexpected happening. We were riding side by side along a country road. The Old Pack had been behaving fairly well, and we were congratulating ourselves that we would soon be in Angus. Suddenly she plunged in between us. Dynamite started bucking and plunging on the left and Black Fairy ran away down the road. A quick glance revealed the fact that Mrs. Beard held her seat and had gained control of her horse, so I gave full attention to mastering mine. Finally I gained control of Dynamite and got the Pack settled down.

Looking back, we saw two badly-frightened young people. They had heard of our coming and, seeing us pass by their ranch, had ridden out to overtake us. Riding up suddenly, they had frightened Pack, which started all the trouble. They felt very sorry, and we told them that we would forgive them only on the condition that they ride with us for awhile, that we might get acquainted. This, of course, was the very thing they had come out to do.

When we rode into Angus, we found another ghost town. Back of our camp was a deserted lumber yard, fast disappearing under a luxurious growth of brush and weeds. In front of us was a bank building falling into ruins. There was still one store remaining. It, with the post office, is run by some fine, generous people.

As the sun went down that night it had broken through the clouds long enough to fall upon a clump of goldenrod and bathe it with glory. But the glow did not last long. With darkness came another severe electric storm, followed by heavy rain throughout the night.

The road next morning was rather slippery and hard to travel, but we did not intend to go far, only to reach Oak. This Nebraska town is immediately on the Old Trail. Many stirring events occurred here. Near by was the famous Narrows, where three men and one woman had been killed by the Indians and a little girl, Lora Roper, had been carried into captivity.

It is related that a man who had come into some little authority in a wagon train, had wantonly killed a young lad riding on one of the wagons, and then in turn was himself killed and buried here. It is said that in the Narrows between hill and river lies a stage coach that had plunged into the water off the slippery ledge; still there today buried beneath the sands.

We heard too the story of Oak Grove Massacre of August 7, 1864. Mrs. Jim Moore, a descendant of the people who owned the Oak Grove Ranch, where the killings had occurred, told us how one of her ancestors had been hidden in a flour barrel and had escaped the bloody hands of the Indians. A fine monument erected here tells a part of that story.

Here at Oak, Dale Kincannon, George Campbell and Eugene Follmer took us out to visit the Trail markers, the place of the Blue Station, the Boy Scout cabin, and the grave of Parson Bob, government contract scout from 1870-1880. As we stood amidst the tangle of grass that marked the resting place of the latter, we read his legend on the stone,

PHILLIP P. LANDON
PARSON BOB
PLAINSMAN
SCOUT
PREACHER
1870-1880
BORN APRIL 15, 1846
DIED NOVEMBER 22, 1933

After reading the inscription, we listened to this story from Mr. Follmer's lips: "Some years ago, an old plainsman, claiming to have been a Government Scout, came through this part of the country, trying to locate the place where he had his lookout point. It was near a spring which was close to this place. With him and several others, we scouted here and there, but for a long time without success. All the time he kept telling the story of Calamity Jane. When about to give up the quest, we came upon the spring. Like a flash, the whole contour of the country became familiar to the old man. Here he had stood behind some trees and had watched the Indians, who were totally unaware of his presence. Here he had often stooped to drink. From this spring he had carried the water to cook his frugal meals.

Then, as he told the story, the old man's hands began to shake, he leaned against one of the trees, the tears rushed from his eyes, great sobs came from his heart, as he exclaimed, "Here was the happiest time of my life, I had my little girl with me then, my little Calamity Jane. I loved her as a father loves his daughter. What a good little girl she was. Yes, she was a good woman, whatever men may say."

When he became calm, he told the men who were with him, this story of her life. Her mother had married a soldier, and, contrary to orders that no woman at any time could be brought to Fort Laramie, he had brought her there.

The soldier was discharged and had to leave the fort, taking his bride with him. Shortly after this, little Calamity Jane was born. Not long afterwards, in an Indian attack, the mother had been shot through the eye by an Indian arrow. As the arrow was pulled from the eye, the mother had died. Just then they heard a cry from the little child, who had been hidden under the floor, to escape the eyes of the Indians. Someone at that time, looking at the dead mother and at the little babe, exclaimed, "What a calamity," and thus the name, Calamity Jane, was given to the unfortunate waif.

Parson Bob took charge of the little one, cared for her, made her clothes, adopted her as his own, and took her wherever he went. He reiterated that she never was a bad woman. She was always going about helping someone and had died from pneumonia, caught from falling through the ice, somewhere near Deadwood, South Dakota, while on an errand of mercy.

When the old man had told this story, he asked Follmer if he would promise to see that he was buried here when he died. Very shortly after this, the old man passed beyond the range. They looked up his record of service with the government and found that he had told the truth. There he was accordingly buried and there we stood looking and musing, while the bees were singing their summer song above the tangled grass of his grave.

When we left Oak next morning, it was without breakfast, for we were to have breakfast with Miss Myrtle Moore at her home some two miles out of town. Afterwards we went out to the Oak Grove Ranch, the scene of the massacre. A great monument marks the place. When we arrived at this, it was to find a gathering of many citizens, who were as interested in the history of the Trail as we were ourselves.

In spite of our late start, and the time consumed at the monument, we made the twenty-five miles to Hebron that afternoon and were given the privilege of camping in the city park. The citizens came out for a friendly picnic as they had done at Oak.

The place was free of mosquitoes, the blue grass was tall and abundant, and the horses had a real picnic. They had never been more contented on the journey. As for ourselves, that park at Hebron became the Happy Isles. We would not have been much surprised to see the great Achilles or even Jim Bridger himself coming to meet us through the leafy trees, over the carpet of richest blue.

Many friends gathered around our campfire that evening. We spent the darkening hours in jest and song and stories. All the earth was benign. Life was full and good. The singing of the frogs which had been joining in the chorus, was sweet. When we stood to bid our parting guests good night we noted that the black blue vault was studded with stars of burning, glowing silver. Earth was crammed with heaven. We uncovered our heads, we lifted up our hearts, we thanked Him from whom all good things come.

When we left Hebron, the chief of police was there to lead us out by the marker that tells the tale of Old Fort Butler, and to get us on the right road. Even then, we got the directions mixed, traveled two miles out of our way, and had to back track. This is one of the hardest things that a rider on the trail can experience. It seems so useless. When it happens, the rider always blames his own carelessness. However, in spite of our mistake, we rode about twenty-eight miles that day.

The road became very monotonous, but the heavenly-blue morning glories, the purple solidity of the iron weed, the buffalo moss, with its five red petals, and the song of meadowlarks more than compensated.

As we entered Fairbury, a young rancher, W. L. Shane,

rode up and invited us to his ranch. We had accepted his invitation and had the Old Pack all unloaded, when Clyde Moore, the editor of the newspaper, and Robert Lee, his photographer, came out to meet us. They had looked for us on another road. They informed us that the Chamber of Commerce had rather special plans for our reception and that we must go on into town. So they kidnapped Mrs. Beard and took her on into Fairbury, where the dinner was to be held.

Frank Kanocke, a deputy sheriff, and a good rider, got on Black Fairy and we rode the horses out to the fair grounds, where one of the horsemen took charge. He informed us that we were not to have a care about them until we were ready to ride away. So we duly, and somewhat relieved, forgot them until Sunday morning.

On our way into town, we saw the quintuplet calves. They are two years old now, fine and strong, with international names, England, Russia, China, America, France. The mother's name was Old Glory and the father had been called Father Time. There was no race suicide in this grand old family.

Fairbury is a thriving city, set amidst attractive surroundings. You feel a sense of its civic pride when you come into contact with its citizens and as you ride through its streets. The chief of police called at the hotel early Sunday morning to take me out to see how the horses were doing. As we rode together, we could feel the pride of the city in the pride he felt as one of its officers. Every thought of the editor, Mr. Moore, was of this city, his city. The ministers, too, were proud of it's open air auditorium, the place for great civic meetings. I was proud of it myself, when privileged to speak to a great, united church gathering in that auditorium on Sunday evening.

In the beautiful park stands a restored cabin of the early days, around it a pool and a great waterwheel. Near the city is the grave of George Winslow, and near it lie buried some forty Mormon folk who succumbed in one of the serious epidemics that swept along the Trail.

Eight miles southeast of Fairbury is Quivera Park, made famous by the fact that Fremont and Kit Carson camped here on June 22, 1842, and carved their names on the face of the jutting rock. We visited this park, driving down about a mile of weed-lined road to a small meadow along a creek. We passed our hands over the face of the cliff, and we can truthfully say that we felt again that delicious thrill of hero worship we had once known in childhood. Both Fremont and Carson had been our early heroes. We had indeed ridden back into the morning of our youth.

It rained all night and was still raining when we left Fairbury at eight o'clock Monday morning. But we had got so used to riding and singing in the rain that it seemed no hardship whatsoever to ride the twenty-three miles to Lanham on the Kansas border.

It was raining when we started, it was raining when we arrived at Lanham. It was raining when we pitched our tent. It was raining, and raining hard, when, standing in it, I ate sweet corn on the cob. My only complaint was that it was hard to keep the butter on the corn while I ate it. We camped in the pasture belonging to William Wieters, the postmaster, who provided delicious sweet corn for his people — guests and rich pasture grass for his horse guests.

Leo E. Dieker, editor of the Hanover *Democrat*, took pictures of the camp in the rain. The thunder rolled, the lightning flashed and the rain came down all night long. But a good tent makes a fine home in any downpour.

We were all fresh and rested when we rode out of Lanham to Hanover, where we ate lunch and from where we rode with Mr. Dieker to the Hollenberg Ranch and Pony Express Station, built in 1857 and called the Cottonwood Station.

Before we left Hanover, the horses, when they became frightened at an incoming train, tried to wrap themselves around some telegraph poles and a car or two. Here we were met by Mr. and Mrs. Dougherty, editors of a Marysville newspaper, and by J. G. Ellenbecker, who gave us an invitation to occupy a little log cabin, and told us how to reach it on our way to Marysville. Mrs. Guys, a reporter from another Marysville paper, accompanied us out to the Hollenberg Ranch. Our visit at the Cottonwood Station or Hollenberg Ranch, was brief, just long enough to visit every room, climb the stairs, and view the sturdy construction of hand-hewed logs. They were rugged builders in those far-off days. If this structure is restored and cared for, as these precious historic buildings should be, it will last for many years to come and will be for inspiration and instruction to countless generations of young Americans as yet unborn.

We kept as near as possible to the Old Trail into Marysville, and in the evening we came to the Last Log Cabin built on the Old Trail, just two miles out of Marysville. The cabin had been our objective for some days. Mr. Ellenbecker had given us such a hearty invitation to make it our headquarters while in Marysville that we approached it as if it were our home. It has a great fireplace, and tables and chairs of hewn timbers. It was surrounded by a rustic fence, but with a gate wide enough for the horses to enter.

Daniel Boone, Kit Carson and Jim Bridger would have felt much at home here. The very pictures on the log walls were all of the plains, the forests, the mountains of the West, of cowboys, traders, Indians.

We unsaddled and turned the horses loose, to go madly tossing their heads and leaping and bucking through one hundred and sixty acres of wild hay meadow. We took the panniers into the cabin and from them just a few necessary articles, then entered the car of Mr. Ellenbecker and rode into Marysville for dinner with himself and wife and the mayor, Jack Beveridge and wife. At the hotel that night we were visited by many people who were interested in the Old Trail and in us, its latest riders.

On Wednesday morning we were taken to all the historic spots around the city. Joe Ellenbecker, like his brother John, now deceased, has always been greatly interested in the Old Trail and in the history of Marysville. Joe was the first man to start experimental feeding of ground corn cobs, as supplementary feeding for cattle. The agricultural colleges of several states are now making successful experiments with this feed.

Through his efforts, the old Perry Hutchinson Mill, first built in August, 1862, was rehabilitated and set to work again. It now employs same fifty people. This man has done much in every way to arouse interest in historic Marysville and to preserve its historic spots for posterity. He was our guide and sponsor through the time of our visit. He took us first to the postoffice, where hangs a remarkable picture of the Pony Express Station, established at Marysville in 1860. The painting was first sketched out by John Ellenbecker and was then painted by D. Vernon Monrose. Marysville had the first postoffice established in Kansas·

Here at Marysville several of the trails came together. Here passed the old Mormon Trail, here came in the trail from Fort Leavenworth, and here the emigrant crossed the Big Blue River. A few miles below Marysville was the famous ford on the Oregon Trail known as the Independence, Mormon or California Crossing. Here thousands of covered wagons with settlers bound for Oregon, Mormons bound for Utah, and gold-seekers for California crossed the river.

In 1849 Frank Marshall, in the face of constant danger from the Indians, established a ferry and trading post at Marysville. Two years later, the Military Road between Fort Leavenworth and Fort Kearney crossed the river at the site of the present Marysville.

Here Marshall established another ferry, and for several years handled the immense traffic. He gave the name of his wife, Mary, to the town that grew up on the site. He gave his own name to Marshall County. In 1860 Marysville became a station on the Pony Express Route, and for most of the 1860's, it was an important point for the great Overland Stage Coach travel.

The first house built in the county was that of Frank Marshall, down by the river near the crossing. We found this old home inhabited by Mrs. Bell, whose father was a great friend of Buffalo Bill. He had ridden with Cody in a parade in Marysville the year that Cody was sixty-six years old. We are still very near our ancient history.

From the Marshall home we drove down the river to noted Alcove Spring, about seven miles south of Marysville, a park-like place in the cup of the hills. Around the spring there had been plenty of grassy space for the wagons, making it the favorite camping place for the travelers before they crossed the Big Blue· Here they rested and recuperated, then drove on to the river and into the hills of the West. Here from under shelving rock, a clear, cold stream still flows. Here thousands of men and women and little children, tired and thirsty with the long journey, had paused and had knelt to drink. Here, too, upon my knees — and it was more as a prayer than for a drink — I knelt and buried my face in its cool depths. Arising, I looked down, and, at my feet, I saw a name carved in the rock,

J. F. REED, MAY 26, 1846.

I read it again and yet again. What was it about this name I was trying to recall? Then, suddenly, it came to me. Reed was one of the members of the the ill-fated Donner Party.

Asking Mr. Ellenbecker if this were so, he replied that it was, and that not far away, Mrs. Sarah Keys, the mother-in-law of J. F. Reed, had died and had been buried; and that two little girls, Patty and Virginia Reed, survivors of that party and granddaughters of Mrs. Keys, each had a lock of her grandmother's hair still pinned in their dress bosoms when they arrived at Fort Sutter in California.

The Donner party reached Alcove Spring near the Big Blue in May, 1846. While waiting to get across the flood-swollen river, the grandmother Sarah Keys died on May 29 at the age of seventy. We were shown the place where she lies in eternal rest beneath the friendly oaks.

Even as we write this story, we have received the welcome information that a beautiful limestone marker with bronze plaque has been prepared and will soon be erected above the grave of this emigrant mother. The stone weighing something like one ton was taken from the historic campsite of the Spring.

So through the labors of men like Joseph Ellenbecker, Gerald Stewart, and Arthur McNew and the vision and splendid purpose of the Arthur Barrett Chapter of the Daughters of the American Revolution, the long delayed honor has been given to Sarah Handley Keys, daughter of a Revolutionary soldier, heroine of the winning of the West.

On the stone will be engraved the words,

God in His love and charity has called
In this beautiful valley a Pioneer Mother

Is not such a place as Alcove Spring sacred? Sacred because of the stream of life that flowed by the silver, trickling rill. Sacred because of the hopes and fears and the pains of the human heart which it has seen and known. Perhaps someday this hallowed bit of ground will be set apart, improved and dedicated to the heroic souls who, passing by, stopped here to rest, to rejoice, and perhaps to pray.

That night we went back to the Last Log Cabin by the side of the Old Trail. A great number of men and women, interested in the storied past of the Trail, came out, and, around that open fire, many tales of the pioneer days were told and retold. Do you suppose that many of those who had passed by in the early days, returned that night and hovered listening to us telling the story of their brave, strong lives?

The next morning we were formally welcomed into the city of Marysville. We rode our horses through to the court house. Here we heard an address and made one. Then, saying good-bye to Mr. Ellenbecker, our kindly host, we rode on down to Blue Rapids.

We had dinner with the Rotary Club, passed through Irving, where we were met by the mayor and state senator and were directed on to Bigelow. Here we received a long distance phone call, asking us when we expected to arrive in Independence.

Here at Bigelow, we were back on the Old Trail again. Here the travelers were wont to pause and lay in a supply of hickory for axe-handles. Here they would prepare to cross the Black Vermillion. From here, we would be able to keep fairly near where the Old Trail had run, until we reached our destination, Independence, Missouri, whence it had started.

XV

THE CLOVER LEAF

"IF YOU ARE LOOKING FOR A GOOD camping place and a good pasture, stop at the Clover Leaf just outside of Topeka." These were the last words that came to our ears from Joe Ellenbecker, as we rode out of Marysville.

All day we rode south over the rolling hills of Kansas, through a sparsely-settled country, rejoicing in the gorgeous purple of the iron weed which grew in every ravine. Nine days remained of our ride.

As we went singing past a ranch house, we were rather startled by a voice at the gate, "Chaplain Beard".

"Yes", I said, reining up.

"Chaplain, we know who you are, and would greatly appreciate it if you would stay with us for a few minutes. Why not stop and have dinner with us?"

My first impulse was to excuse ourselves and continue on our way, but then I remembered that we were really in no hurry. "What do you say?" I asked Mrs. Beard.

She replied, "Why not?"

A young fellow took care of the horses and we entered the ranch house of a French soldier in the First World War who had come at it's close to America, the land of promise.

That night we camped in the American Legion ball park at Westmoreland. Next morning by twelve o'clock we entered and passed through Wamego· We rode out by the Dutch Mill, an ancient structure which had been removed from it's original foundation and brought into Wamego.

This day we rode thirty-two miles, passing several fields where hail had practically mowed down the corn. A good, strong wind blew through most of the day, so we were free from the pest of flies and mosquitoes.

As we entered St. Mary's Mission, a loud speaker greeted us with a hearty welcome. Here the citizens, in preparation for the Centennial of the Founding of St. Mary's Mission on the fourth, fifth and sixth of September, were all dressed in the costumes of a hundred years ago. We were conducted to the city park, and were told that it was ours and to camp anywhere we pleased.

We chose a place under a great oak that must have been standing when the Mission was founded. It had stood there through the sunshine and storms of a century apparently without a broken branch but shortly before we arrived it had been struck by lightning and cruelly blasted. It was slowly but surely dying. How strange is fate, even the fate of trees.

We spent the Sabbath day of August 8 at St. Mary's. Crowds of men and women and little children came around to visit us. They were especially curious about the horses and gathered like flies to talk to them and pet them. The horses seemed to like it, and even Black Dynamite did little more than stand and switch his tail.

Around our campfire that night we had the usual group of old-timers, interested in the Old Trail and in us who were riding it. We heard some new stories of dangers met and difficulties overcome, and some old tales in somewhat different garb and detail. One we had heard away out on the Tygh Creek in Oregon. An old man told it to us, saying that it was told to him by his mother who'd come over the Trail sometime between 1843-49. The tale was so unusual and seemingly so impossible that we gave it little credence, but, hearing it again at this end of the Trail, we began to think it may have been true. It seems that in one of the smaller groups of wagon trains there was a pretty little girl of some thirteen or fourteen years of age. A group of Ogallala Sioux had visited the train and had ridden along with it for several days, and one of the young braves had fallen madly in love with the child. Some one in the train had unscrupulously promised the young Indian that, for a certain number of horses, he could have the girl for his bride. The young brave rode away across the prairies but soon returned with the fixed number of ponies, but when he asked for the girl, she could not be found. Her parents had got some inkling of the bargain and had hidden the child under the bedding in one of the wagons. It seemed for a time that the train would be attacked by the infuriated Indian and his friends but he was finally appeased with bountiful gifts. When the Indians were gone, they found the unscrupulous knave who had made the bargain, and, with the use of the great bull-whips, drove him from the camp and out on the prairies. No one ever knew whether he lived to make the journey or not. It is said the family of the little girl came through safely.

While in this park, we witnessed a square dance put on by the Riding Club, all costumed and on fine horses. It was very beautiful. We would like to have ridden with them but the horses needed their Sabbath day rest.

Sunday night, a delegation of men, Newton Weir, Herb Boydson, and Don Sullivan from the Chamber of Commerce and the riding club, came out to make arrangements for our reception in Independence. They asked us to try to make it there by August 14. This was just one day before our appointed schedule to come to the end of the Trail, but we promised that we would do it. And, like the Little Red Hen, we did.

We had heard so many tales of the early days in Kansas from our grandmother's lips, about Marysville, the Crossing of the Blue, the Smoky Hill River, the Flint Hills, the Old Shawnee Mission and St. Mary's Mission, that we seemed to have come, ourselves, to old well-known places. Every place was entered with great expectations, visited in naive wonder, and left with utmost reluctance.

It was with real regret that, on Monday morning, August 9, we rode out of town, past the old Mission buildings and took our way toward Topeka and the Clover Leaf, and the early crossings of the Kansas.

Early in the evening, in fact, at four o'clock, we rode into the Clover Leaf, that intricate fabric of curving concrete roads that give a swift and safe automobile entrance into the Capitol city. In every curve and bend, we found what would have made a fine camping spot. We camped where the road straightened out and ran directly into town. We had hardly arrived when we were greeted by newspaper men from Topeka and Kansas City.

We picketed the horses and made arrangements to have some oats sent down from the city, then pitched the tent on a high ridge of ground, and prepared to rest for the night.

It was well we had been accustomed to put the tent on high ground, for the next day, while visiting the historic spots of the city, a storm of cyclonic proportions struck a section of Topeka, blowing down many trees, wrecking many autos, and sending down a deluge of water. When we returned to camp, we found the horses standing belly deep in water and mud and seemingly wondering what it was all about, but everything in the tent was snug and dry. There is real science in tent-pitching.

Early in the morning we were taken to the capitol building and had a happy visit with Governor Frank Carlson. Later we went with Kirke Mechem and George A. Root, of the museum, for a visit out to old Union Town and to the first crossing of the Kaw River.

About five miles out of Topeka and near the Old Crossing stands a stone house of the Baptist Mission established in 1848. Geery, appointed territorial governor by Buchanan, made a trip in 1856 to this section to pacify the Indians, stopped here for a week, and made a Thanksgiving proclamation.

Nothing is left of old Union Town but a tangled graveyard where twenty-two Pattawatomie Indians lie buried.

At the Clover Leaf in Topeka we spent two wonderful nights and a day, and at eight o'clock on Wednesday morning we rode out and away toward Lawrence.

This hot day was tempered by a great field of red clover through which we rode. The horses came in good and strong and we pitched camp alongside the road where the Red Teepe Inn stood just outside Lawrence.

XVI

END OF THE TRAIL

"The End of the Trail", they call it, that sculptured figure by Earl James Fraser, of the lone Indian on his spent pony. The horse's head hangs low. The tired, hopeless rider looks sad, defeated. The end of all things seems to have come to horse and rider alike.

The end of the trail was likewise in sight for two white Indians on the Old Trail but I am sure there was no dejection or sadness shown in their faces. For this End of the Trail had been their dream for years and was the Mecca of four and a half months of hard and continuous riding, ever into the Sunrise.

We spent a trying, restless night camped there at the corner of the highway by the Red Teepe Inn. The Kansas night was so hot that we could not sleep in the tent and was so full of mosquitoes and other insects that we could not sleep outside of it. Gladness and regret mingled in all our thoughts this night. We were glad success seemed so near. We were sad that soon we would be saying good-by to the little tent. This was to be our last night in it.

Next morning we were up at five as usual and broke camp at eight o'clock. The horses were eager to be off. They, too, had been restless all night long. I rode off without my spurs, the first time I had ever mounted Black Dynamite without them. Guess he did not know it, for he gave no more than the usual trouble to mount and, when, after riding a quarter of a mile, I turned back for them, it was on a run. We rejoined the party on a run and pulled up in a cloud of dust. He enjoyed the canter, and it seemed to shake the kinks out of our very bones. We turned in for breakfast at a fine eating place down the road, and, joy adding zest to our appetites, we were soon fortified for a hot, hard ride.

Here the Pack, running true to form, broke loose, and in doing so wrecked her halter. Today it was just riding on hot pavement or riding off on the shoulders, when possible. It was a case of hide and seek, dodging cars.

Knowing that we would reach Kansas City next day, Mrs. Beard suggested that we better find an auto camp for the night, in order to wash and get cleaned up for the entrance. So our camping out was over.

We had just got nicely settled when it began to storm. This, too, was in harmony with the trek. Rain, rain, rain!

In the middle of the night, we were awakened from a dream-filled sleep by a crash of thunder. I had been dreaming of that weazoned-up little shrimp of a cowpoke. He had just ridden up alongside as we were turning into camp.

"Well, " I said, "this is Victory Camp."

"But," he replied, "you will find tomorrow's ride long, hot, hard and dangerous, I know I could make it, but I don't think you can."

"Why, you good-for-nothing, dirty, little, weazoned-up shrimp", I answered, "I'll bet my good two-bladed jack knife I can ride the very pants off you". Then, leaning across the saddle, and, standing in one stirrup, I swung for his jaw. As my fist landed, the crash of thunder came, and he vanished back up the road in a cloud of smoke.

Dreams are strange things. Sometimes, in a dream, even a minister may find his true self revealed.

On this, our last day of the ride, we started in the rain; but we also started singing our old marching song, which we had composed while riding through a terrible storm of rain, hail, snow, and sleet along the Trail on Farewell Bend in Idaho.

And the skies did soon clear as we rode into Kansas City. We were met by Mr. Woodard, the president of the Chamber of Commerce of Kansas City, Kansas, a group of newspaper men, and several policemen. Throwing up my hands at sight of the latter, I exclaimed, "Now, what have I done? Of course I have broken your speed laws, for when the notices have read RESUME 35 MILES AN HOUR, I just couldn't do it".

"Chaplain", said the policeman in charge, "you have done nothing, but we are going to do something. We are going to see that you get through the traffic of Kansas City".

So, escorted by these fine men, some in front and some at the rear, we rode through the city and across the long bridge over the river.

As we came out upon the bridge, we looked across its far reach to the heights above. The scene was so striking and beautiful, that we asked our escort if they would pause till we could view it for awhile. "Take your time, Chaplain", they replied, "we are at your service".

It was mid-afternoon, some few sprays of smoke were rising

over the heights from the railroad yards along the river, the rays of the westing sun were weaving these smoke wisps into splendid tapestries that hung down from the tall, graceful buildings above. As we lifted our eyes to the enchanting beauty of the city on the hill that could not be hid, we seemed for a time in an unreal world of fancy and of dreams. Again we moved on. And now we were met by a group of policemen from Kansas City, Missouri, who escorted us through their city and to it's border. Here Mrs. Harmon Russell met us, a very picture of youth, grace and loveliness on her splendid horse. She escorted us to her home, where we were to be entertained during our visit in Independence. The horses were turned loose on the spacious, bluegrass lawn.

It was still early afternoon. Mrs. Beard, when told of the plans for our reception in Independence next day, expressed her desire for some new clothes to fit the occasion. So we were taken by Mrs. Russell for a shopping trip back to Kansas City. It truly seemed good to mingle again with the shopping crowd, though somewhat awkward to walk in the high-heeled cowboy boots. We had ridden so long that we had almost forgotten how to walk.

A little fellow, next day, catching Black Fairy by the bridle, looked up and said, "You've come a long ways, haven't you?"

"Yes," said Mrs. Beard, "about twenty-five hundred miles."

"And you have ridden all that way?"

"Yes".

"Gosh, aren't you afraid you'll be bowlegged when you get off?"

"Oh", laughed she, "I think not, I'm used to it".

Then he said, "I know a lot of fellows who have ridden a long way, and they are all bowlegged".

That night, Mrs. Beard, standing as straight as an arrow, turned around and around, two or three times, and said to me, rather wistfully, "I'm not bowlegged now, am I"?

I did not dare to put myself to such a test. I felt bowlegged, I felt stiff-legged, and I felt awkward, following the two women on that shopping trip through the stores of Kansas City, and was greatly relieved when, after buying new hats, belts, rainbow scarfs, white satin shirts, and riding boots, we returned to the peace and security of our host's home.

Our entrance into Independence, the goal of our long ride and the starting point of the Old Oregon Trail, is an event that will never be forgotten. Certainly a heart-warming reception had been prepared.

At ten o'clock, a large group of men and women, all in gorgeous Western costumes and mounted upon spirited horses, rode up to the gate, gave us a hearty welcome, then ordered us to fall in behind the colors, as we started for the heart of the city. Immediately back of us, came a little covered conestoga wagon, drawn by Shetland ponies and driven by a man in the dress of a plainsman. Then back of this the long double line of riders.

Ahead was an escort of policemen on motorcycles, then came the mayor and officials of the city government. There was stirring music, as through the streets, thronged with people, we wended our way past the President's home and up to the Old Court House, where over a hundred years ago, the Old Oregon Trail had started.

The whole square was packed with happy, smiling people who gave us a royal welcome. Mayor Roger Sermon made a short speech, reemphasizing that welcome. Just in front of a great sign which read, THE OLD TRAIL STARTED HERE, we had our pictures taken. After the exercises in the city square we returned to the Russell home, took off our saddles for the last time, packed them for shipment back home, and turned the horses out in pasture for a good long rest.

We washed up and rested, and, in about an hour, we were taken to the hotel to a sumptuous banquet. About two hundred guests were present. Newt Weir, president of the riding club, presented Mrs. Beard with two beautiful bronze horses for book ends and the president of the Chamber of Commerce presented us both with a framed picture of President Truman. On this picture the President had written, "Congratulations to Chaplain and Mrs. Beard upon their trip on horseback over the Old Oregon Trail". Herb Boydston crated this fine picture and sent it by express to our home in Portland, where, greatly cherished, it hangs over the radio for all to see.

After the banquet, we were taken in official cars for a tour of historic things. In the old days, Independence was noted for it's four springs. Three of the springs are now dry, but one is still sending out it's life-giving stream.

Cave Springs is a remarkable thing. All of the emigrants stopped here. The stream of water comes out of a grotto, above which is a great and old hackberry tree. By bending down one can follow the grotto back for a hundred feet — some say for two blocks — to a chamber about twenty feet square.

Red Bridge Farm, on the original Santa Fe and Oregon Trail, once a trading post is now owned by Brice B. Smith, former mayor of Kansas City. The bridge is still painted bright red, thus carrying on the old tradition.

Down in the pasture near the river, close to some trees, we found an old broken gravestone. It had once marked the spot where two men, Isaac and Alexander Paxton, had been murdered, while waiting to cross the river. A better monument marks the grave now. It is a large walnut tree, which is rooted in the graves.

These men were murdered one night by a man whom they had befriended. He then took their wagon and horses and drove on into California· Years later, the man who then owned the ground, received a letter from a hospital in California, where the murderer lay dying. He had confessed the deed and told where his victims lay buried. Excavation at that point uncovered their remains.

The first crossing of Blue River at this place on the Santa Fe Trail was by fording. The first bridge was built in 1861 by a man named Todd, who, it is said, had killed a man in England and then fled to America.

George Todd, the son, was a Lieutenant under Quantril and later was a major in the Confederate Army.

From this place we were taken down the road on which Price's Army marched from the Battle of Westport. On the way we heard some good words said for Quantril, the only time in all the years that I have heard such.

We next visited old Mt. Washington Cemetery at Kansas City, to see the grave of Jim Bridger. We found it in a secluded spot, looking out over a green plot of ground gemmed with many trees, a place resembling nature as Bridger must have known it. On the great, gray stone are the words,

"JAMES BRIDGER
1804-1881
CELEBRATED AS A HUNTER, TRAPPER, FUR TRADER AND GUIDE
DISCOVERED GREAT SALT LAKE IN 1824
THE SOUTH PASS IN 1827
VISITED YELLOW STONE LAKE AND GEYSERS IN 1830
FOUNDER OF FORT BRIDGER IN 1843
OPENED OVERLAND ROUTE BY BRIDGER'S PASS TO
GREAT SALT LAKE
WAS GUIDE FOR U.S. EXPLORING EXPEDITIONS
ALBERT SIDNEY JOHNSTON'S ARMY IN 1857 AND
G. M. DODGE IN U. P. SURVEY
IN INDIAN CAMPAIGNS 1856-66
THIS MONUMENT IS ERECTED TO HIS PIONEER WORK BY
MAJ. GEN. G. M. DODGE"

Mr. Kemper, the county clerk of Jackson county, told us of wolves and coyotes, once infesting the prairies and groves around Independence. He said further that the coyotes are still a problem to be dealt with, 160 scalps having been brought in the past year.

We next visited the spacious depot in Kansas City, Missouri. In the Westport room are two striking murals, Westport Landing, by Meier, and Pawnee, by A. Edgar Miller.

From here we were taken to see a log cabin built in 1821. The large house, standing near by, built in 1844, was called the Manor Home. The vast estate on which these stood had been bought for one dollar an acre when John Quincy Adams was President of the United States.

Now we were to reach the real Mecca of our dreams, the Shawnee Mission. Many of the tales told to us in our childhood had centered around this old Methodist Mission, built in 1839. It was immediately on the Santa Fe and Oregon Trail. Troops in the war with Mexico had marched by its walls. Caravans for Santa Fe and the Southwest had lumbered along, sending clouds of dust over its windows and roofs. Thousands of covered wagons, bound for Oregon and California, had passed through it's grounds, where the paved highway now runs. At least 100,000 Forty-niners, perhaps saying a little prayer for success to crown their search of gold, had wistfully bade it good-by as they passed its friendly portals to ride on and on.

That night a colorful street dance was held in the public square. Literally thousands of folk jammed the streets. They were dressed in the costumes of the wagon train days and danced the old square dances often danced by the emigrants at night, when the trains were drawn up in great circles on the plains. Old time music was played and old time songs were sung.

Independence, Missouri, was back that night in it's Frontier Days. And we who had ridden the Trail were there with it.

In our long ride we had looked for the spirit of America, when men had dreams and had matched their strength to make the dreams come true, and the spirit of America had traveled with us along the Old Trail.

We had looked for adventure and we had found thrilling adventure on every mile—fording rivers; threading mountain passes; crossing desert stretches; fighting gnats, flies, mosquitoes; riding through rain and crashing storms.

We had looked for romance and had found it in the stories we heard along the way.

We had looked for beauty and we found it in wild flowers; in the spreading wings of birds; in cloud-armies marching across the skies; in the desert nights; on the lonesome plains; in mountain ranges; in the beautiful cities arisen since covered-wagon days.

We are glad that we could take our saddles and ride east together over the Old Oregon Trail—that riding east we could ride into the sunrise, and into our youth again.

INDEX

K

Kanocke, Frank, 155.
Kansas, 150, 158, 161, 163, 165.
Kansas City, Kansas, 163, 166.
Kansas City, Missouri, 98, 104, 165, 167, 169, 170.
Kansas River, 163.
Kanseau, 83.
Kaw River, 164.
Kearney, 139, 143, 145.
Kearney, Miles, 129.
Kemmerer, 93, 94, 102.
Kemmerer *Gazette,* 93.
Kemper County Clerk, 170.
Keys, Sarah, 159.
Kincannon, Dale, 152.
Klickert, Doris, 74.
Kline, Milton, 143.
Klip Creek, 10, 16.
Klondike, 34.
Koger, Dr. L. M., 56.
Krebs, John, Donna, Coleen, Dick, 37.

L

Ladd Canyon, 50.
Lafayette County, Missouri, 146.
LaGrande, 48, 49, 50.
Lage, Ed and Mable, 26.
Landon, Phillip P. (Parson Bob), 152.
Langrell, Etha, 52.
Lanham, Kansas, 156.
Lapwai, 137.
Laurel, Nebraska, 149.
Laurel Hill, 14, 149.
Laramie Creek, 127.
Lawrence, Kansas, 164.
Lazy-Man's Ranch, 149.
Leavenworth, 84.
Lee, Daniel, 21.
Lee, Jason, 8, 18, 21, 22, 46, 47, 83, 114.
Lee, Robert, 155.
Lee, Rev. T. Samuel, 45.
Lewis and Clark, 7, 22, 104.
Lexington, 141.
Light, Jennie, 146.
Lime, 54.
Lincoln, Nebraska, 145.
Lloyd Ranch, 90.
Lloyd, Sr., 89.
Louis, Joe, 121, 122.
Lowell, Nebraska, 146.
Lugenbeil, Major, 61.

M

Mahanaim, 40.
Mantor, Dr. Lyle, 143.
Marmot, 13, 14.
Marshall County, Indiana, 150, 158.
Marshall, Frank, 158.
Marshall, Mary, 158.
Marshall Station, 44.
Marysville, 156, 157, 158, 160, 161, 163.
Massacre Rocks, 80, 81.
McAllister, P. M., 52.
McArthur, Lewis A. 44.
McKay, Tom, 56, 57.
McKay, Dr. William, 44.
McGrew, 113.
McIntosh, J. L., 113.
McLoughlin, Dr. John, 8, 13.
McLoughlin, Margaret, 8.
McNew, Arthur, 159.
McNulty, Alda, 140.
Meacham City, 47.
Meacham, Walter, 30.
Mechem, Kirke, 164.
Meek, Joseph L., 9, 12.
Meeker, Ezra, 83, 107.
Meeker, Ezra, Springs, 48.
Meier, William, 145.
Meier, Artist, 170.
Memaloose Island, 22.
Merritt, G. A., 35.
Mexican Hill, 126.
Middleton, 44.
Mexico, 93, 170.
Miller, Edgar A., 170.
Miller, Peter, 123.
Milner Dam, 70, 71.
Minden, 139, 140, 144, 145, 146, 149.
Missouri River, 71, 129.
Mitchell, 130.
Mitchell Pass, 130.
Moeller, Mrs. E. B., 52.
Moffett, Howard, 74.
Monrose, D. Vernon, 158.
Montpelier, 89.
Montana, 37, 71.
Moore, Clyde, Editor, 155.
Moore, Mrs. Jim, 152.
Moore, Myrtle, 153.
Mormon Trail, 125.
Mt. Adams, 26.
Mt. Hood, 9, 14, 26, 79.
Mt. Putnam, 58, 79, 85, 86.
Morrison, Clint, 130.
Mountain Home, 62, 63.
Mueller, Fred A., 145.
Murry, Eunice Hunt, 53.

Other titles in the Equestrian Travel Classic series published by
The Long Riders' Guild Press. We are constantly adding to our
collection, so for an up-to-date list please visit our website:
www.thelongridersguild.com

Title	Author
Southern Cross to Pole Star – Tschiffely's Ride	Aime Tschiffley
Tale of Two Horses	Aime Tschiffley
Bridle Paths	Aime Tschiffely
This Way Southward	Aime Tschiffely
Bohemia Junction	Aime Tschiffely
Through Persia on a Sidesaddle	Ella C. Sykes
Through Russia on a Mustang	Thomas Stevens
Across Patagonia	Lady Florence Dixie
A Ride to Khiva	Frederick Burnaby
Ocean to Ocean on Horseback	Williard Glazier
Rural Rides – Volume One	William Cobbett
Rural Rides – Volume Two	William Cobbett
Adventures in Mexico	George F. Ruxton
Travels with A Donkey in the Cevennes	Robert Louis Stevenson
Winter Sketches from the Saddle	John Codman
Following the Frontier	Roger Pocock
On Horseback in Virginia	Charles Dudley Warner
California Coast Trails	J. Smeeton Chase
My Kingdom for a Horse	Margaret Leigh
The Journeys of Celia Fiennes	Celia Fiennes
On Horseback through Asia Minor	Fred Burnaby
The Abode of Snow	Andrew Wilson
A Lady's Life in the Rocky Mountains	Isabella Bird
Travels in Afghanistan	Ernest F. Fox
Through Mexico on Horseback	Joseph Carl Goodwin
Caucasian Journey	Negley Farson
Turkestan Solo	Ella K. Maillart
Through the Highlands of Shropshire	Magdalene M. Weale
Wartime Ride	J. W. Day
Across the Roof of the World	Wilfred Skrede
Woman on a Horse	Ana Beker
Saddles East	John W. Beard
Last of the Saddle Tramps	Messanie Wilkins
Ride a White Horse	William Holt
Manual of Pack Transportation	H. W. Daly
Horses, Saddles and Bridles	W. H. Carter
Notes on Elementary Equitation	Carleton S. Cooke
Cavalry Drill Regulations	United States Army
Horse Packing	Charles Johnson Post
14th Century Arabic Riding Manual	Muhammad al-Aqsarai
The Art of Travel	Francis Galton
Shanghai à Moscou	Madame de Bourboulon
Saddlebags for Suitcases	Mary Bosanquet
The Road to the Grey Pamir	Ana Louise Strong
Boot and Saddle in Africa	Thomas Lambie
To the Foot of the Rainbow	Clyde Kluckhohn
Through Five Republics on Horseback	George Ray
Journey from the Arctic	Donald Brown
Saddle and Canoe	Theodore Winthrop
The Prairie Traveler	Randolph Marcy
Reiter, Pferd und Fahrer – Volume One	Dr. C. Geuer
Reiter, Pferd und Fahrer – Volume Two	Dr. C. Geuer